The publisher of this book is generously donating all royalties from the retail sales of **"REMARKABLE RETIREMENT 03"** to:

LEMONADE DAY

America was built on the back of small business. Entrepreneurs take risks believing they can realize their dream if they work hard, take responsibility and act as good stewards of their resources. Today's youth share that optimism but lack the life skills, mentorship and real-world experience necessary to be successful. In 2007, founder Michael Holthouse had a vision to empower today's youth to become tomorrow's entrepreneurs through helping them start, own and operate their very own business… a lemonade stand.

Lemonade Day is a strategic 14-step process that walks youth from a dream to a business plan while teaching them the same principles required to start any big company. Inspiring kids to work hard and make a profit, they are also taught to spend some, save some and share some by giving back to their community. Since its launch in 2007 in Houston Texas, Lemonade Day has grown from serving 2,700 kids in one city to 1 million children across North America. With the help of partners like Google for Entrepreneurs, Lemonade Day will continue to spark the spirit of entrepreneurship and empower youth to set goals, work hard, and achieve their dreams.

You can learn more about Lemonade Day by visiting:
www.LemonadeDay.org

REMARKABLE RETIREMENT

America's Leading Retirement Advisors Speak

VOLUME 3

By Remarkable Press™

Remarkable Retirement Volume 3/ Mark Imperial. —1st ed.

Managing Editor/ Stewart Andrew Alexander

ISBN-13: 978-1-7323763-0-4

CONTENTS

A NOTE TO THE READER

Thank you for buying your copy of **"Remarkable Retirement Volume 3: America's Leading Retirement Advisors Speak."** This book was originally created as a series of live interviews, that's why it reads like a series of conversations, rather than a traditional book that talks *at you.*

I wanted you to feel as though the participants and I are talking *with you,* much like a close friend, or relative, and felt that creating the material this way would make it easier for you to grasp the topics and put them to use quickly, rather than wading through hundreds of pages.

So grab a pen, take notes and get ready to learn some fascinating insights and real-world experiences about retirement planning.

Warmest regards,

Mark Imperial
Author and Radio Personality

INTRODUCTION

"Remarkable Retirement Volume 3: America's Leading Retirement Advisors Speak" is a collaborative book series featuring leading Financial Advisors from across the country who are passionate about helping retirement planning.

Remarkable Press™ would like to extend a heartfelt thank you to all participants who took the time to submit their chapter and offer their support in becoming *'Get the word out Ambassadors'* for this project.

Remarkable Press™ has pledged 100% of the royalties from the retail sales of this book to be donated to Lemonade Day.

Should you want to make a direct donation, visit their website at: www.LemonadeDay.org

JOHN AMATULLI, CFEd® RFC®

Financial Advisor

Amatulli and Associates Financial Services

Email: amatulliandassociatesfs@yahoo.com
Website: www.amatullifinancialservices.com
LinkedIn: www.linkedin.com/in/john-amatulli
Call: (855) 723-6669 (SAF-MONY)
Call: Indiana Office (219) 365-5544
Call: Illinois Office (224) 735-2234

John Amatulli is a Certified Financial Educator. John is the president of Amatulli and Associates Financial Services. John assists people retired or nearing retirement with their financial needs. John teaches other financial professionals and offers Retirement Planning workshops for the public throughout the Indiana and Illinois areas.

John has always been a caring person. He loves people and loves taking care of people. His financial practice serves over 450 clients. John has served on the board for the State of Indiana Better Business Bureau (BBB) for 10 years. He has also served on the board for the Chicago Children's Hospital.

When John was sixteen to his early twenties, he played on the racquetball pro tour. He has won several state and national titles for the sport. In 1996, John won a silver medal in the Olympics for the sport of racquetball.

John has three children, two girls and a boy. He enjoys working around the house outdoors, fishing and likes to be on the water. He says it his therapy.

Indiana University is where John attended school and graduated with a major in Finance and a minor in Marketing. He also went to the School of Financial Planning in Denver.

At the end of this chapter, John gives the story of why he became a financial advisor.

THE JOURNEY TO PEACE
OF MIND IN RETIREMENT
By John Amatulli

Tell us about Amatulli and Associates Financial Services, the clients you work with and the types of situations they find themselves in when they come to you for your help?

I founded Amatulli & Associates Financial Services with the philosophy that I always place the needs and interests of my clients first.

I help people on the verge of retirement or already retired to increase their wealth, so they can keep their hard-earned investments and have peace of mind in retirement.

Many people that come in to see me are nervous about their money. My goal is to take out the confusion and mystery, which seems to surround the financial world. I explain the main financial dilemmas that threaten financial peace of mind. I teach people how to overcome these dilemmas in simple enlightening terms. I create a plan for my clients that allows them to sleep well at night knowing they have specific guarantees on their money.

My primary focus for my clients is to receive more income, attain more growth, pay less tax and leave more money for their spouses, children, grandchildren and any other of their beneficiaries.

When a potential client comes to me, I take a financial snapshot of their portfolio and investment situation. I then determine whether they need help with estate planning issues and whether there is too much exposure to unnecessary taxation. I also establish whether there is too much potential market risk in the portfolio-too much equity with no potential to fluctuate quickly depending on the mood of the market.

Lastly, I often make suggestions resulting in less exposure to taxes, especially after death. Also, I commonly make suggestions to reduce exposure to the markets, particularly the equity markets. By lowering taxes and risk, I may be able to raise the value of the portfolio. The result for my clients, while living and after death, is a bigger estate for family and loved ones.

What are the advantages of increasing wealth for the people you work with?

I would say the biggest advantage for my clients is eliminating the financial stress, worries and fears about their money. Often, clients will tell me, "John, I wish we could have met you years ago. You are the first financial advisor where we understand what you are saying and the recommendations you are suggesting."

Other advantages of increasing wealth for people is they can sleep better at night. They have peace of mind when it comes to their money. While increasing my client's wealth, I often put their money into accounts that are guaranteed. Personally, I am a conservative advisor. I am not a gambler.

Nor will I gamble with my client's hard earned money. The accounts I use have the ability to pay out an income stream in retirement. This is like having a paycheck for life. It is a way to create a "personal pension plan" for my clients. The solutions I recommend create confidence leading up to retirement and during retirement.

What do you feel are the biggest myths out there when it comes to your investments in retirement?

There are a lot of myths out there when it comes to money, investing, taxes and retirement. Over the years, I've learned that these myths and misconceptions about investments and money seem to be the same no matter who I'm working with.

The biggest myth that I've found in all my years, is that most people believe that they have to keep their money in the market enduring all of the ups and downs to make money for retirement. They do not realize that there are accounts out there that can eliminate the losses when the market goes down. They also do not realize or believe that it's not truly about the size of their portfolio, it's about the income they can get during their retirement for their lifetime.

Retirement is not complicated, so when I teach at the university, conventions and workshops, I break it down to simple steps that folks can understand. The true success of your retirement is based on the income that you can receive over the years. Unfortunately, most investors, people retired or nearing retirement, and stockbrokers don't understand this philosophy.

What are some common misconceptions around the Finance industry?

There are many misconceptions about the finance industry. I believe that one of the biggest misconceptions is that some folks think they can pick their own investments and manage their own portfolio.

Most folks do not have the time or expertise to do the necessary research required to manage a portfolio. To see positive results, one would have to watch their portfolio like a hawk and make experienced decisions.

I often see another misconception. Some people believe you cannot lose money in bonds. That belief is 100% false. Bonds and interest rates have an inverse effect on each other. When interest rates decrease, the value of bonds are higher.

When interest rates rise, the value of bonds are lower. Currently, interest rates are historically low. Interest rates have risen recently and are expected to rise. Therefore, if you have bonds, you may consider a review of your account in a consultation I provide.

What are some of the most common fears about money in retirement?

The most common fear that I see is people fear running out of money in retirement!! The fact is, that because we are all living longer, we need to have more money to last in retirement. Approximately, 51% of Americans are nervous that their nest egg isn't going to be enough for retirement.

Some folks fear that Social Security will be reduced or not be around for them in retirement. Normally, Social Security replaces approximately 40% of a worker's pre-retirement income. According to the Social Security Administration, nearly half of single seniors count on it for at least 90% of their income.

Another fear is getting seriously sick where long-term care is necessary. Long-term care is very expensive. It is not covered by private insurance or Medicare. The financial toll of that care is staggering and devastating to one's financial well-being.

I have plans and accounts that work as a long-term care solution. It is a hybrid type of investment that offers a long-term care component. Rather than paying expensive monthly premiums, you pay a lump sum into an account that acts like a savings account.

At a time when you may need funds for long-term care, the dollar amount can triple for benefits. This plan is an alternative that many of my clients take advantage of. This way you can have a safe investment with the ability to cover much of the long-term care expenses.

What should people on the verge of retirement or already retired do to get past those fears?

Most people don't pay close enough attention to their retirement portfolio until they are close to retirement or already retired. I say it's never too early to plan. Get with a financial advisor or planner that you can trust and start the process.

For those still working, I would suggest that they add more money to their retirement plans. This should be done consistently such as a monthly contribution. Especially, if it can be done through payroll deductions, you don't miss the money as much. For those already retired, pay down debt, especially high-interest debt.

I would also suggest that folks have a social security illustration done from an advisor or planner. This will tell you how to optimize and get the most money from social security in your lifetime.

The other item I highly suggest is that folks have some type of plan for long-term care. There are plans out there that you pay a single premium into to cover long-term care, and if you don't get sick and use your benefit, you can get the money out with interest in your lifetime, or a loved one would get it as a death benefit.

What other perceived obstacles do you see that might be preventing the people you work with from seeking the help of a Financial Advisor?

I would say the number one thing is "change". Most people that are older don't like to change, even if they know or feel it would be better for them and their loved ones. A lot of clients I have worked with over the years have been working with their current advisor in some cases for many, many years and would feel uncomfortable leaving them.

They also fear the transfer process and don't want to take the time, or worry that their current advisor will get mad at them. I always tell people, don't do what's in my best interest, or your current advisors best interest!! You should think and do what's always best for you and your family.

At Amatulli and Associates Financial Services, we do everything possible to make the sure the financial transition is seamless. We stay in touch with our clients every step of the way to make them feel comfortable.

What are some of the little-known pitfalls or common mistakes you see people make on the road to retirement?

There are many common mistakes I see people make on the financial road to retirement. Financial planning for retirement takes time and discipline. A comfortable retirement savings does NOT happen overnight! It takes regular consistent contributions and possibly sacrifices. An analogy I use is exercise and getting in physical shape. To reach a weight goal takes time. One has to watch their diet and exercise regularly to see small benefits over time. At some point in time in the future, a goal is met. Once the goal is met, then the challenge is consistency. Saving and financial planning for retirement is no different.

I often see people not making contributions to their Individual Retirement Accounts, "IRA's" or their 401K plans. Some people put this off until the following year. Then the following year comes and it happens again. The next thing you know is ten or twenty years have gone by. You should at the very least contribute what your company may be matching in your workplace retirement plan such as a 401K. Time is valuable when it comes to building a nest egg.

Another mistake I see is people do not look at or review their quarterly or annual statements. You should have at least a good understanding of your investments. In the event you do not, I can be of assistance. As a Certified Financial Educator, I offer Retirement Planning Workshops regularly at libraries, universities, community centers and local restaurants.

A big issue I run across in my financial assessments is people accumulate too much debt. I can offer advice on how to reduce debt and create a plan of action with you.

I offer a complimentary assessment to answer questions about retirement plans. During these sessions, I will make recommendations to place you on the right track. My recommendations will allow you to meet reasonable financial goals. Some of these goals may be accumulation, safe money, or income. If your goal is income, for example, I have plans that will allow you to generate an income stream in your retirement years. Please feel free to take advantage of this educational opportunity to overcome and avoid common financial pitfalls.

How can these pitfalls or mistakes be avoided?

Many financial pitfalls can be avoided by having the right guidance. A financial advisor like myself will act as a coach for your finances. Even top professional athletes need a coach. Michael Jordan had a coach. Tiger Woods in his prime had a coach assist with his golf swing. Using the services of a good, ethical financial planner to assist with important financial decisions is highly recommended.

As your financial planner who has been on the board of directors for the Better Business Bureau in the state of Indiana for the past 10 years, I commit to doing things in your best interest. By using my recommendations, many pitfalls can be avoided.

I have a requirement to become a client. You must make an agreement to meet with me in person at least one time a year to review your statements and portfolio. Why do I do this? Maybe I am not so good at doing this over the phone. I prefer you come into my office with your financial statement in front of you. As your advisor, I receive copies of your financial investments. I like to go through the statement line by line. By doing this, I find that people understand their investments better. I want you to understand your investments better because it is your money and it is important to you!

Share an example of how you have helped someone on the verge of retirement or already retired to overcome those obstacles and succeed in keeping their hard earned investments.

Tom and Mary came in to see me and were very nervous and uncomfortable about their upcoming retirement. I took them through a very easy fact-finding mission. I asked them simple questions that they knew the answers to without looking up information.

We discussed their goals in retirement and how they wanted to spend it. I then came up with a plan for them, explained it in simple English terms that they could understand. I believe in keeping things simple so everyone understands what I'm recommending for their money and how they can live their lives without running out of money.

After our initial meeting where I gathered information, I was able to analyze Tom and Mary's answers. I did some research to develop the right plan to meet their goals. At a follow-up meeting, I presented a plan using an account that acted like a pension.

Tom and Mary are now able to "turn a switch" and generate an income stream they cannot outlive. They are able to defer the income to a time in the future. The longer the deferral period, the higher the income will be. Therefore, I was able to help Tom and Mary so they can make their own decision and control their income in retirement.

What inspired you to become a Financial Advisor, what's your backstory?

When I was young, I was playing on the men's pro racquetball tour and teaching at my own racquetball camps. At that time, I made some decent money for a young person. My dad and I knew a financial advisor at the club we played racquetball with. This advisor/friend was with a well known national brokerage house. He lost 80% of my money within a year and a half!!! Keep in mind, this was All of my savings!!! I couldn't believe it. I later found out he was not our friend and put the money in high-risk funds that paid the highest commissions.

I decided then I eventually wanted to become a financial advisor so this would not happen to anyone else. I realized that this was happening to other older people at the club I knew and played ball with. They didn't have the time to wait for the market to come back. These people depended and needed to live on this money.

I get up every day and work to protect the financial portfolios of people that come to see me. This is one of the reasons why I became a financial advisor. My advice gives my clients the peace of mind they deserve to live a successful retirement.

What's the most important thing people on the verge of retirement or already retired should consider when evaluating a Financial Advisor?

I believe that the most important thing is trust!! The client should believe and feel that they trust the advisor. I always tell folks that I meet with, if it doesn't feel right in your gut, then don't do it.

Be sure to ask the advisor any and all questions that you have, so you get a thorough feel for this person.

What are your final thoughts for people who want to keep their hard-earned investments and never run out of money during retirement?

People who want to keep their investments and never run out of money should consult with a conservative advisor who specializes in working with people retired or nearing retirement. The advisor should have credentials, an office, clients and a positive reputation. One of the investments that is often suitable for retirees or those approximately 50 years of age or older is a Fixed Indexed Annuity. I am a big fan of the Fixed Indexed Annuity.

You may have heard annuities are bad. Not this one. The fixed indexed annuity gives you principal protection!! This means that when the stock market goes down, you do not lose any of your money nor the interest that you've earned. I tell my clients, we all love making money. I have never met anyone yet that likes making money and then give it back when the stock market goes down. This account can also be set up to use like a pension. It has the ability to give you a pension for life so you never run out of money.

When you come to see me for a no fee, no obligation meeting, I will determine if this account would be in your best interest.

If someone feels they want to increase their wealth, so they can keep their hard earned investments, how can they connect with you?

Anyone can feel free to contact me at this number: (855) SAF-MONY 723-6669 or log on to our company learning center: www.amatullifinancialservices.com. I also would welcome you to attend one of my retirement workshops to learn more about topics concerning retirement. I also offer a no cost, no obligation meeting at one of my offices in Indiana or Illinois to see if I have any recommendations for you.

I have no minimums as a financial advisor. My belief is that if you help people and do good things for people it comes back to you. I also believe, if you do bad things, it will eventually come back to you as well.

I'm proud to say that last year was our best referral year ever. This makes me feel really good inside. When my clients are passing my name on to their family, loved ones, and friends, they must think I'm doing a good job for them and have their best interest at heart.

EUGENE COYLE CFP® ChFC®

CERTIFIED FINANCIAL PLANNER™
Coyle and Associates Financial Services, LLC

Email: eugenecoyle@sbcglobal.net
Website: www.coyleandassociates.com
LinkedIn: www.linkedin.com/in/eugene-coyle
Call: (847) 736-7954 | **Fax:** (224) 735-2596

Eugene Coyle is the president of Coyle & Associates Financial Services, LLC. As a CERTIFIED FINANCIAL PLANNER™ practitioner and Chartered Financial Consultant, his personal practice specializes in working with baby boomers and retirees. Eugene places an emphasis on "Safe Money," while advising his clients on insurance, estate planning, annuities, money management and income tax strategies.

As a fiduciary, Eugene has conducted hundreds of Retirement Planning Workshops over the past 17 years throughout the Midwest. Since 2005, he had responsibility for and a leadership role in growing a start-up agency to over 200 financial professionals. Eugene is also one of the founding principals of Advisors Circle Financial & Insurance Group, LLC. At Advisors Circle, he educates and trains other financial professionals with finance and marketing.

Eugene often travels throughout the country conducting continuing education courses for financial professionals. As president of Coyle & Associates Financial Services and Advisors Circle Financial & Insurance Group, LLC, Eugene realizes giving back to his clients and other financial professionals is a recipe for success and he has a proven track record of doing so.

YOUR MONEY, YOUR RETIREMENT
By Eugene Coyle, CFP® ChFC®

Tell us about Coyle and Associates, LLC, the people you work with and the types of situations they find themselves in when they come to you for your help?

I help baby boomers and retirees to keep their hard earned money, so you can retire financially comfortable, knowing you will never run out of money.

Coyle and Associates Financial Services is a company that works with people nearing retirement or retired. A focus I have for prospects and clients is to help educate you on your finances. Why? Because so many people come into the office to meet with me and they do not really have a good understanding of their investments. In fact, I have worked with clients through two major market corrections in 2000-2002 and 2008-2009. Some people have come into my office during those poor market conditions where they did not open their financial statements. Could you imagine not opening your own financial statements? These people and others need to be put on the right path where they do not have fear. Rather, you need to be able to sleep comfortably at night knowing the bulk of your money is safe from market downturns.

People come to me for financial assistance with a variety of situations. One of the biggest concerning situations regarding your money in life is your fear of running out of money. I have recommendations that are appropriate for many retirees to avoid worrying about running out of money. These recommendations solve this problem. For example, if you are retired and have a pension and social security, you know exactly how much monthly income you will receive for the rest of your life. At Coyle and Associates Financial Services, I have investment accounts that resemble a pension. Therefore, if appropriate, I can open an account for you to assure you will have the financial comfort of monthly income for life. This will eliminate the fears that often come with people and their money.

What are the advantages of keeping hard earned money, for baby boomers and retirees?

There are numerous advantages to finding the right financial advice. When looking for advice, you need to do your due diligence. I recommend seeking out the services of a CERTIFIED FINANCIAL PLANNER™ professional. At Coyle and Associates, I have the credentials to provide advice on income tax, investments, estate planning, insurance and more. I have a fiduciary responsibility to act in your best interest and my clients best interest. This is something that may not always prove to be true in the financial industry.

Some people have a "gut" feeling and an emotional response when discussing their money. These people are more expressive, outgoing and willing to share their emotions about their money. Others think in a quantitative or analytical way. These people want to see numbers and spreadsheets. Which type of person are you? Regardless of emotional or analytical thinking, my goal is to make you feel comfortable. With that goal comes education. I want you to learn enough about your money to make a sound financial decision when investing. Once this decision is made, you should feel comfortable knowing the money you worked so hard for, will now be working for you. The desired outcome is to keep your hard earned money and for you to have peace of mind when it comes to your money.

What do you feel are the biggest myths out there when it comes to keeping your hard earned money?

You may have heard many myths when it comes to your money. For example:

Have you ever heard to keep your money invested in the stock market because it is guaranteed to grow over time?

The stock market can be volatile. There are no guarantees with the stock market. As a conservative financial planner, I believe as you get older, you should reduce the amount of money you have at risk. A simple rule I use is called the "Rule of 100." This means you can take your age and subtract it from 100. The answer is the most amount of money you should have at risk. For example, if you are 65 years old, the equation to determine the most amount of money you should have at risk is 100 - 65 = 35%. Therefore, in this example, 35% is the most amount of money you should have at risk. I use the word "risk" to cover stocks, bonds, mutual funds and other investments that may go down in value.

You should accumulate debt to increase your credit.

Accumulating debt is not the way to increase your credit. Rather, paying off your debt is a way to increase your credit. I recommend if you have credit cards, you should be financially responsible and pay off your debt monthly. By paying off your debt consistently, your credit will be strong and sound.

Do not pay off your home mortgage.

One of the advantages of owning a home is deducting the mortgage interest. Keep in mind the mortgage interest is a cost that comes out of your pocket! If you have the opportunity and savings to pay off your mortgage, it may be something for you to consider.

Keep your money in the stock market through your retirement to maximize returns.

You should consider reducing the money you have in the market at retirement. Why? Because you want to have the security knowing the money you have worked so hard for will be there without gambling in the market. There are numerous ways I assist people nearing retirement or retired without investing in the stock market. One of the methods I use is an investment that allows some of the gains of the market with no downside risk. The negative is you do not receive ALL the gains of the market. The positive is you do NOT lose any money when the market goes down!

I don't have enough money to invest.

You should consider "paying yourself first." What I mean by that is when you receive income, you should set aside a consistent amount for your own personal investment. Then you can pay your bills with the remainder. This is discipline you should implement to assure you will accumulate your own savings and investment plan. At times this is easier said than done!

Regardless of the myths you may have heard, saving and keeping your hard earned money takes practice and consistency. I can assist you with a budget or plan so you can have comfort knowing your money will be there for you throughout your retirement.

What are some common misconceptions around the Finance industry?

There are numerous misconceptions in the financial industry. You may think it is too late to start investing enough to reach your financial goals. I believe it is never too late to start saving / investing for your retirement. You may have to make some sacrifices and work longer. However, starting now is better than never starting. By starting now, you can positively impact your financial retirement.

Another misconception I often hear working with planning for retirement is you can count on a 4% return from your investments in retirement. Therefore, if you have accumulated one million dollars, you can be assured you will receive a 4% return or $40,000 annually, without tapping into your one million dollars. Unfortunately, there is NO guarantee for a 4% return. We are experiencing a low interest rate environment and a volatile stock market. An interest rate return number that may be more likely is 2.8% to 3%. Therefore, I recommend you do not count on a guaranteed 4% return on your investments in retirement.

I often hear one should invest in the stock market and over time the market will grow. You may ask yourself, "Will the stock market continue to grow when I need my money?" The issue is when you decide to withdraw funds from the market. At that time, possibly upon your retirement, the sequence of returns is most important. For example, if you retired in 2000 with your savings in the market, and begun to withdraw income, you would have experienced a "Double Decline" with your money.

What do I mean by "Double Decline?" While you were withdrawing money, your account value was declining by that amount you withdrew. Additionally, your account was declining due to market declines. This continued to happen for that decade from 2000-2010, with two major market declines. One in which the market experienced approximately a 40% decline in 2008!

Regardless of these misconceptions and more, I recommend for my client's true diversification with some "safe money" to assure your money will be there when you need to rely on it.

What are some of the most common fears about people losing their hard earned money?

Let's face it, one of the fears you may have is, "Will I have enough money for the rest of my life?" You have probably worked hard your whole life and saved what was feasible. It is natural to second guess and ask yourself, "Is this enough money to last me?" Or you may ask yourself. "What if this doesn't work?" Another question you may have is, "How will this affect me in a negative way?"

You may even fear the amount of time, knowledge and time commitment it will take to get it right. The good news is if you are reading and taking note of my message here, you are taking steps to place yourself in a positive financial position. It is never too late to plan or prepare when it comes to your finances. The earlier you begin, the better the chance you have to succeed.

Seeking the services of a CERTIFIED FINANCIAL PLANNER™ Professional is a great start. More than likely, you have had teachers or mentors in life. Financial planning is no different. You may want to consider verifying if you are on the right path. Or, you may already be working with a financial person. It doesn't hurt to get a second opinion. Therefore, if you are on the right track, I will tell you that you are in a good position financially. You can go home and sleep well knowing the person you are working with is doing the right things for you. However, I often see areas that need to be addressed or have not been addressed. This is where I can make some recommendations in your best interest as a true fiduciary. By taking this step, you can rest assured overcoming your fears about losing your hard earned money!

What should baby boomers and retirees do to get past those fears?

You may get past your potential fears about your money through education and asking questions. There is an abundance of information on the internet, at libraries, local universities and financial seminars you can attend. Step one is gathering information. Through your research, you may want to establish a relationship with a financial planner like myself. Initially, you will experience a consultation. During this consultation, I have a "Fact Finder" where I ask you questions. These are simple questions you will have the answers to. This is where I gather information. An analogy I often use is similar to going to the doctor. You must go through a sample of tests while the doctor performs a physical evaluation.

Following the evaluation, the doctor will determine if you have any physical issues that need to be assessed further or treatment. Your financial consultation works the same way.

Once the information is gathered, I spend time analyzing and evaluating the answers you have given to me on your fact finder. This will allow me to determine whether I have a recommendation for you or not. More importantly, if I do have a recommendation, it will be in your and your family's best interest. As a CFP®, I have a fiduciary responsibility to act in your best interest when making financial recommendations.

At another meeting, I will illustrate and explain my recommendations. If you like my recommendations, we may proceed. If not, we do not need to take action. At the very least, you have educated yourself further on your financial situation. If you do feel positive and make a decision to proceed, I will lead and implement the necessary steps to take action. Following the implementation of the plan, I will monitor your accounts on a regular basis. This will make you feel comfortable knowing your financial plan is in a positive situation and alleviate any fears you may have.

What other perceived obstacles do you see that might be preventing people from seeking the help of a CERTIFIED FINANCIAL PLANNER™ Professional?

Some people think they do not have enough money or they are not sophisticated enough about their money. Others do not allocate the time necessary to meet with a financial professional. In fact, it is often stated that some people take more time to plan their vacation than their financial retirement.

Keep in mind, when I need eye care, I go to a vision care specialist. OR when I need an estate plan, I seek the services of an estate planning attorney. If I need assistance with my taxes, I use a Certified Public Accountant. Financial planning is no different. If you need financial recommendations, you should seek the services of a CERTIFIED FINANCIAL PLANNER™ Professional.

Another obstacle you may have is the cost involved to hire a financial planner. I personally offer a complimentary financial assessment. I do not charge a fee because I do not know if I can help you with your finances. Upon review of your finances, if there are financial investments I like, I will tell you and you may keep them there. In the event I can assist you with areas of concern or areas I can improve upon, I will explain in simple detail so you can understand. At times, I am compensated directly by a company rather than my clients. Therefore, there may be no cost to implement a plan. I am usually able to help most people I see with some of their money.

When it comes to keeping their life savings, what are some of the common pitfalls and mistakes you see baby boomers and retirees make?

One of the most common mistakes I see baby boomers and retirees make with their money is placing the needs of others such as family in front of their own financial situation. A common mistake is to invest in their children's and grandchildren's education rather than having enough invested for their own retirement. My recommendation is to make sure you have enough money for you and your spouse first. Then, you may invest or gift to your family. For example, those of you who travel, it is recommended in emergency situations to place your oxygen mask on yourself first, then you are capable of assisting others such as your children. Saving for your financial retirement works the same way. You must be in control of your finances. Therefore, you do not have to worry about someone else providing for you. Once you achieve this accomplishment, you may then be in a position where you can financially contribute or gift to others or charities.

Another common pitfall you could make is spending too much on luxuries and not implementing some sort of budget. All too often people live for the now and don't plan for the future. Time is one of the most precious elements of life. Time and finances work well together. The more time you can invest and save, the more financially comfortable you can be in your retirement years.

On the topic of pitfalls, some people rely on their financial advisors or bank, without really dissecting or understanding their investments. You should be involved with how your money is invested. You should know that the goal or ultimate outcome should be realistic. Another area of interest is the costs or fees you are paying in your account. Are you aware of the fees in your accounts? Fees can take a big bite out of your financial wellbeing.

You should be consistently on top of your money matters to avoid some of these common pitfalls. This way you become more involved. You get to make financial satisfaction a priority!

How can these pitfalls or mistakes be avoided?

Financial pitfalls and mistakes can be substantially reduced or avoided. When you come and see me for your financial consultation, I will ask questions to assist me in gathering information about you and your financial situation. You will be able to inform me about your traits and habits in addition to numbers. Your answers will allow me to determine if I have a recommendation for you. Together, we can come to a conclusion about your financial goals. I may recommend some type of consistent savings plan or a budget to create discipline and consistency. You should allocate some time weekly or monthly to assess your finances. To assure you do not create pitfalls for yourself, you may want to establish regular meetings with a financial planner like myself to keep you on track. This is similar to setting weight or fitness goals. At times, you may need to seek the services of a nutritionist or personal fitness trainer to teach, plan and monitor your health. Financial planning can work the same way.

At some point when you have achieved your financial goals, you may retire or work only because you want to, not because you have to. This is when you may need assistance in determining what money you should draw from to live on. I have assisted many people with creating an income stream in retirement. This income may be a lifetime income, like a pension. You may need advice on how to take this income in the most tax-efficient manner. By doing this, you can potentially avoid another pitfall, which is paying too much in tax.

All of your financial scenarios need to be addressed. When you come and see me, I am often able to assist in giving the advice necessary to avoid common pitfalls and mistakes.

Share an example of how you have helped someone to overcome these obstacles and succeed in retiring financially comfortable.

I have been involved in speaking at "Retirement Planning" workshops and seminars to the public for the past 18 years. Following my presentations, it is common for people to desire more information about my topics. One of the topics I present is "Safe Money" places. During this topic of "Safe Money," I suggest moving some money from risk to safety to avoid a loss of money if the stock market declines. Many attendees schedule an appointment, following my seminar, to come to my office for a complimentary consultation.

Louise came to one of my seminars and scheduled an appointment with me one day back in 2007. Louise was in a common situation I see often. She was retired and a widow. Her deceased husband handled all the finances until he passed away recently. Louise needed advice. She liked the idea of moving some of her money from risk to safety for many reasons. First of all, her husband used to handle the finances. Second, Louise did not know much about the stock market. Third, she liked the idea of safety and guarantees I discussed at the workshop.

Following our positive meeting, Louise wanted to move forward and protect her finances with my suggestions. However, she was not quick to make a decision. She wanted another opinion or two. She mentioned that she would like to discuss my recommendations with her son and her existing financial advisor, who her husband worked with. I wanted Louise to feel comfortable following our meeting. Sure enough, she asked her 45-year-old son who was living with her. He said she should stay the course with Ken the existing advisor. Then Louise asked Ken, her advisor. Ken said you are in a good financial situation and the market has been performing well. You should keep your investments as they are and "stay the course."

I followed up with Louise and she told me she was going to keep her investments the way they are and thanked me for my time and advice. You probably know what happened shortly after 2007. The stock market tanked and dropped approximately 40%! Unfortunately, Louise lost nearly half of her IRA account in the market decline! She tried to get a hold of her advisor. He did not return her calls. When she finally reached her advisor, his response was, "what do you want from me? The entire market is down!"

Louise remembered the meeting she had with me and the idea of "Safe Money." She reached out to me and scheduled another appointment. Louise did finally move some money away from risk to safety with guarantees. She is a client to this day! Now she can sleep at night knowing the money she moved in her IRA can never decline due to market declines. I like to call this "sleep insurance."

This is one of the ways I can help people avoid common mistakes and pitfalls when it comes to investing their hard earned money.

What inspired you to become a CERTIFIED FINANCIAL PLANNER™ Professional?

I have always been interested in finance. During college, I worked for a company that owned and operated health and fitness multi-purpose facilities. I was involved in management making financial decisions while reviewing profit and loss statements as well as income statements. My background in school was finance and marketing. After college, I was mentored by several people in the financial industry. However, being mentored was not good enough for me. Some of these people had experience but not the top designations in the industry. Therefore, I did some research and realized one of the top designations one could obtain in the financial industry is to become a "CERTIFIED FINANCIAL PLANNER™ Professional."

To pursue the CFP® designation was a big decision. At the time, the prerequisites to sit for the comprehensive exam were to pass seven independent financial related courses. Once those courses were passed, I could sit for a comprehensive two day, ten-hour proctored exam, which was offered three times a year.

I decided to move forward and I put in extensive study time. This allowed me to learn about numerous areas such as Investments, Income Tax, Estate Planning, Insurance, and Retirement Planning. Fortunately, I accomplished passing the exam! Additionally, I earned the Chartered Financial Consultant designation. As a CERTIFIED FINANCIAL PLANNER™ Professional, I use my education and experience to truly hold myself out as a fiduciary to assist others with their financial needs.

What's the most important thing baby boomers and retirees should consider when evaluating a CERTIFIED FINANCIAL PLANNER™ Professional?

If you are looking for a financial professional to assist you with your financial needs, you want to look for experience, specialization, qualifications and a designation, such as a CFP® and ChFC®.

Some of these items or qualities may appear obvious. Especially when you are looking for advice with your life's savings. When I use the word "specialization," I reference this word because you want a financial advisor who deals with situations, where someone like you is nearing retirement or retired.

This is similar to going to see a doctor for your knee or hip problems. What type of doctor do you look for? An orthopedic doctor who does knee and hip surgeries week to week. You do not want to go to any general practitioner. You want to seek the services of a "specialist." Financial planning works the same way. Most financial planners work with anyone who has money.

I work with people as a "specialist," in dealing with planning and preparing for retirement. Furthermore, you should choose to work with an advisor who has a designation or is "certified." There is a reason why you may seek the service of an attorney who has the designation, "Juris Doctor." That person has a certification as an attorney. Or you may want an accountant to review your tax situation. The type of accountant you should look for is one who has achieved certification such as a Certified Public Accountant or CPA. When you look for financial recommendations, my recommendation is to seek the services of a CERTIFIED FINANCIAL PLANNER™ Professional.

What are your final thoughts for baby boomers and retirees whose goal is to be financially comfortable in retirement?

If you are reading this you are to be commended for doing your own financial due diligence. Finding the right plan for your money can be a challenge. Who do you trust? What is the right course of action? How do you get there? All these questions can be answered by choosing the right financial planner to assist you. I can do this for you!

Sure there is a time commitment. As I previously mentioned, most people spend more time planning for their vacation than they do planning for their retirement. Some people think they can do this by themselves. Maybe they can? Why not use the services of a specialist to double check? Your retirement savings is so important. Knowing the right plan for your money can overcome one of the biggest fears in life. Not running out of money!

Some people think being financially comfortable in retirement is not possible. Others think it is too much of a price to hire a professional. I assure you that being financially comfortable is possible. Now, I cannot make magic. However, I can recommend the best possible plan with the money you have worked so hard for. With respect to price, that may vary. Often, a complimentary consultation is offered. I do this in my practice. Why? Because I don't know if I can help someone or not. Therefore, I offer a first appointment complimentary. My recommendation is to get a second opinion on your finances.

You may think you are comfortable and with the right person handling your finances. There is nothing wrong with getting a second opinion. If I like the plan you are in, I will tell you. If I have a recommendation that will place your money in a better position, I will tell you in simple terms so you can understand. Therefore, ultimately you will make the most educated decision about your money for you and your family.

If someone feels they want to keep their savings, so they can retire financially comfortable knowing they will never run out of money, how can they connect with you, and what will happen when they do?

If you are someone who would like to take advantage of seeking recommendations for your financial retirement, here is my offer. At Coyle and Associates Financial Services, I offer a no-fee complimentary consultation. I ask you to bring in to this meeting all your important financial documents. You may bring any financial statements you receive quarterly or annually. If you have a trust, you may bring it to the meeting. I ask you to bring any documents that show your beneficiaries. I would rather have more information than not enough.

In our first meeting, I will do what I call a "Fact Finder." It is simply one blank sheet of paper where I ask you simple questions. Questions you will know the answers to. The answers will allow me to determine whether I have a recommendation for you or not. More importantly, if I do have a recommendation for you, it will be in your and your family's best interest, not my best interest.

I then take time to analyze and research the questions and answers on your fact finder. At a second appointment, I spend time explaining what you are currently invested in. If there are good areas, I will tell you I like those investments and may recommend keeping those. In the event there are areas I can improve your accounts on, I will explain in simple terms how I can help improve your financial situation.

If you like my recommendations, GREAT! If not, you are the boss. It is your money and ultimately your decision. I am usually able to help MOST people with SOME of their money!

You may contact www.coyleandassociates.com or call Eugene Coyle, CFP®, ChFC® at (847) 736-7954 to schedule your complimentary assessment. I would look forward to assisting you as a fiduciary with your financial needs.

NICHOLAS NARDULLI

Estate Planner

Nardulli & Associates, LLC

Email: nick@ntag-tax.com
Website: www.nardulliandassociates.com
Call: (800) 969-7925

Nick Nardulli is the President and CEO of Nardulli & Associates and the Nardulli Tax Advisory Group. Nick's leadership and thoroughness in the Estate and Tax Planning process is unmatched in the industry.

Serving clients in financial services for nearly 30 years, he is responsible for procuring new clients and maintaining client relationships. Nick is proud of the existing long-term client relationships he has developed over the years.

This team approach for Legal, Tax and Financial services is uncommon in this industry. Retired clients and soon-to-be retiree clients are refreshed to depend on Nick Nardulli and his team at Nardulli & Associates for financial, estate and tax planning.

THE FAMILY DEFINED BENEFIT ADVANTAGE IN ESTATE PLANNING
By Nicholas Nardulli

Tell us about Nardulli & Associates, LLC, the people you work with and the types of situations they find themselves in when they come to you for your help?

Nardulli & Associates is a dedicated Estate and Tax Planning firm. My team and I collaborate with an Attorney and CPA to provide full spectrum, proper planning based on the needs and desires of our clients. We focus on the population between the ages of 50 and over. Our emphasis is on the education of our clients, as we help them understand and navigate through the maze of confusion in Estate and Tax Planning. We use easy to understand language and straightforward, proven strategies.

One of the most common problems for this demographic is the misunderstanding that designating beneficiaries is a solution for Estate Planning. This process of naming beneficiaries properly can have devastating effects if done incorrectly.

We preemptively rectify this and other issues as we design and implement a Family Defined Benefits Strategy for our clients. My team analyzes the client's individual needs and concerns and creates a specialized plan that will work for the family. We stay committed throughout the process so that their assets will smoothly transition to their heirs. The outcome from this defined benefit is a legacy achieved in perpetuity for multiple generations.

What are the advantages of estate planning for the families you help?

Our niche is that we have a team approach towards Estate Planning. We are a multi-faceted organization with a focus to help parents, children, and grandchildren. We help our clients identify their needs, wants and desires for their families and then we work as a team to reach those goals.

Peace of mind comes with knowledge, education and with the support of a team of experienced and dedicated professionals. When we initially meet, we review their current estate and legal plan and identify its strengths and weaknesses. I, as your Wealth Manager, will coordinate your Estate Plan through our Elder Law Attorney, who will offer resolutions using time-proven methods of proper legal documentation, while our CPA works to reduce taxes and to apply long-term tax strategies. Our team works together to create a plan that will benefit our clients for generations to come

The advantages of working with Nick Nardulli and Nardulli & Associates is our team approach towards Estate Planning with respect to all family members.

I will act as your "Wealth Manager" to coordinate your Estate Plan through our Elder Law Attorney. Our attorney will offer resolutions using time-proven methods of proper legal documentation. Additionally, our CPA works to reduce taxes and applies up to date and advantageous tax strategies.

What do you feel are the biggest myths out there when it comes to creating family estate plans?

One of the biggest myths we often hear when it comes to creating family estate plans is, "It is only for the wealthy." You may hear the word, "estate," and think "wealth." However, wealth comes in many forms such as health, families, relationships and more.

Another common myth is, "All I need is a will and to name beneficiaries." These documents are not meant to be static. Rather, they should be fluid as life changes dictate. Most importantly, a will does not provide Estate protection.

Lastly, at Nardulli & Associates, we often hear, "It is only for the elderly." Whether you are 18 years of age or 90, or firm encourages everyone to have some form of documentation in place for their families.

What are some common misconceptions about the Insurance and Finance industry?

A common misconception in the Insurance & Finance Industry is that when you purchase a product and assign beneficiaries, the inheritance is protected and you will not need to have an Estate Plan. But have you asked yourself - "Where does this fit in my family?" "What goals is this accomplishing? "What are its limitations?" In this industry, the customary method of service is to provide products to clients. These products by themselves have inherent limitations in protecting families. Some important points you may consider:

- What happens if one of the beneficiaries goes through a divorce, a bankruptcy, or is or becomes disabled?

- How are their assets being protected?

- What are the family dynamics and how will they come to play when a life event occurs?

These well-intended actions have unintended consequences.

Another common misconception is that your typical financial services firm's approach to "single lane" plans do not coordinate with one another. Individual firms are each driving in their own lane without a direction to reach a common destination. You don't want to be driving the wrong way on a one-way road.

At Nardulli & Associates, I will supervise all plans and assure protection regarding financial, estate and tax planning for you and your family.

What are some of your client's most common fears about estate planning?

Estate planning is not a familiar subject for most people. Not having advanced or even basic knowledge of a topic can be scary and intimidating. This is common for most people but estate planning deals with real family issues. The stakes are high and our clients have a definite fear of making a mistake.

In many cases all our clients have to rely on is the information we present them so it can be very difficult for some to trust we are doing what is in their best interests. Being taken advantage of is another real fear for our clients.

In Estate and Financial planning, stories abound of people losing their retirement accounts or unwittingly appointing financial planners as beneficiaries or straight-out theft from their estate planners. We now know that the large financial institutions themselves are not to be blindly trusted as recent news stories have told us. This leaves our clients in a very difficult spot. Who can they trust? Who is right and who is wrong? Why is their accountant telling them one thing while we are telling them the opposite? It is no wonder our clients have a fear of estate planning with all the noise coming from their various financial professionals. The cost has always been a fear of our clients as well.

Most people think they have to be very rich to need any form of estate planning. When people hear estate planning they most equate it with wealth and think it does not apply to them. Because of this assumption, many think the costs associated with estate planning are prohibitive much less maintaining such a plan. We see this every day with our clients and prospective clients. The fear of the costs and the potential embarrassment they might face if they cannot afford it can be petrifying. In some cases, this prevents people from doing any planning at all which could lead to the worst outcomes. Another anxiety our clients have is of the familial nature.

When doing estate planning one has to appoint people, usually family members as agents for healthcare and property should they get disabled. One also has to appoint who will be the point person to settle their final affairs after they leave this world. This means one is faced with deciding which child to appoint and why. Because this is family planning and not engineering a bridge, feelings are involved. Our clients sometimes dread having to choose between their children for fear of hurting one's feelings. In its true essence estate planning is loving planning. The main reason for doing estate planning is out of love for one's family and the last thing our clients want to do is cause distress or turmoil.

What should the 55-75-year-olds you work with do to get past those fears?

Education… Education… Education!

We hold public workshops that offer an opportunity to become acquainted with myself and our Elder Law Attorney in a non-threatening way. It minimizes that initial concern of that first one-on-one meeting. Our workshop is designed to educate and help people to become comfortable with us and familiar with the process of getting their estate in order. Our Elder Law Attorney educates on the pros and cons of proper Estate Planning. This helps to alleviate common misconceptions & myths.

My focus is on generational succession by using a properly drafted trust as a mechanism for wealth transfer.

Following the educational workshop, we offer at no cost in which our potential clients can discuss their unique dynamics, concerns, and questions in a private setting. We work with them to educate and equip so that they can make the decisions that are most beneficial to themselves and their family.

If I told you, "No ongoing fees," would that calm your uneasiness? As life changes, we are committed to your family. Our Elder Law Attorney has "No billable hours."

What other perceived obstacles do you see that might be preventing 55-75-year-olds from seeking the help of an Estate Planner?

There are several reasons that people don't recognize that they have a need for a personal Estate Plan. Often, they hesitate because they don't want to face their own mortality. This is especially true with us men. It's a fear I used to have. It helps to know that once you have your estate in order, most people feel relieved and free to move on in life.

Another obstacle is having to face the possibility that your current advisor may not have accomplished the goals you aspired for your estate. This is especially difficult when there has been a long business relationship, often 10-15 years. Ultimately, we all want to do what's best for our own family and it helps to have an Estate Planner that represents you on your behalf.

Finally, people are often concerned about the time and effort that will be needed on their part to get the job done. We are all so busy nowadays, even retirees. Our team of experienced professionals and support staff has developed procedures and methods to streamline the estate planning process. Our process is explained in simple terms so you have a good understanding. We will assist you in understanding the plan as it is important to you and your family. Our team will make sure this is done in a time-saving manner for you. I and my team will promise to be available to you as our client in the future and as life presents its changes and challenges.

When it comes to creating estate plans for their families, what are some of the common pitfalls and mistakes you see 55-75 year olds make?

Most people do not understand that a named beneficiary is an irrevocable decision once a person has passed away. If a named beneficiary on a savings, checking or investment account goes through a life event such as a divorce, bankruptcy, has special needs or becomes disabled, that asset may be at risk. Proper Estate Planning will provide protection.

Another pitfall we come across is incomplete Estate Plans. For example, when all the assets have not been connected to a trust, an incomplete Estate Plan will not perform.

At Nardulli & Associates, my team and I will review existing plans and work with you to create a thorough, complete plan. By delivering a proper Estate Plan, we can prevent some common pitfalls and mistakes.

How can these pitfalls or mistakes be avoided?

A qualified second opinion would reveal if a client's goals were or were not attained. When you work with our team of professionals, all your Estate Planning needs are met. Our multi-generational Elder Law Attorney reviews legal documents with a focus on current laws. Recommendations are made to bring the documents up to date.

Our seasoned experienced team will then review the current assets and verify with the various institutions that they are connected to their documents.

By educating our clients on the process, allows them the understanding and importance of the procedure and what is involved. Our annual review process ensures education on the continual steps involved in Estate Planning.

I educate my clients on our process. This allows my clients to understand the importance of our procedures and what is involved. The education process continues for you during our annual reviews. You are involved in the continual steps to assure you have a thorough understanding of your Estate Plan.

Share an example of how you have helped someone to overcome those obstacles, reduce risk and get their affairs in order.

Several years ago, a husband and wife came to our firm through one of our workshops to get a proper Estate Plan done. They recognized that the plan they already had in place did not meet their needs. Our professionals reviewed their documents and by our recommendations, the entire estate plan was rebuilt to their wishes. They wanted to ensure the protection of the estate for the surviving spouse, once one passed away. They were especially concerned about land and some investments that were not in a tax-favored position.

We were able to revalue all their assets so that the surviving spouse would be able to sell them and not worry about taxes. Proper Estate Planning helps minimize capital gains tax when one spouse passes away. A few years later, the husband died and because the new plan was in place, the wife was spared capital gains taxes. We were able to increase the income to her property by 100%. Again, this is what proper Estate Planning accomplishes. Now she has peace of mind knowing that with our team as her ally, we have her and her family's best interest at heart.

Another situation comes to mind – A retired couple recently came to one of our workshops and heard about Special Needs Trusts for the first time. This caught their attention because they have a teenage grandson with special needs. Our Elder Law Attorney, being well versed in this area, amended their existing trust to incorporate his needs. This created a separate Special Needs Trust for the grandson so he can maintain his government benefits. This prompted the couple to notify their son and daughter-n-law that they needed to get their Estate Planning done.

The couple has expressed to us several times the relief they have knowing that their beloved grandson will be taken care of and they are definitely enjoying their retirement. This is Multigenerational Faceted Estate Planning at its best. This is why we do it!

What led you to become an Estate Planner, what's your backstory?

I got into the insurance business in 1988, working with Pioneer Life in Rockford, Illinois. Next thing you know I am learning about Medicare and Medicare Supplemental Insurance. I kept hearing the same questions form my clients. - "What's a Will?" "What's a Trust?" "How do I protect my assets?" "How do I save on taxes?", things like that.

In an effort to help my clients navigate through the labyrinth of Estate Planning, I partnered with an Elder Law Attorney and we began to present Estate Planning Seminars throughout the state of Illinois. We continued to do that for seven years together and I can tell you I learned more in those seven years than I did in college. One story that comes to mind is a family in Southern Illinois that owned 885 acres of farmland. With the attorney's guidance, we were able to preserve the capital gains for the surviving spouse and family.

I also discovered my passion for helping people in Estate Planning. I love introducing the possibilities before them. I love helping them reach their goals, especially when facing a challenge. In the 27 years that I've been doing this, I have never come across a situation that our team, working with the client could not resolve.

We continued to present seminars for seven years together. I can tell you I learned more in those seven years than I did in college.

What's the most important thing 55-75-year-olds should consider when evaluating an Estate Planner?

The experience of the Attorney, the Wealth Manager, and the CPA. Consider their years in the field. At Nardulli & Associates, we are not PRACTICING on our clients.

I have been coordinating between Elder Law Attorneys and CPA's since 1990, designing Family Defined Benefit Plans. We have numerous examples of Estate Plans that are working today in multigenerational fashions that have withstood the test of time.

Remember when you are considering someone as an Estate Planner, you are not just evaluating them for yourself, but for generations to come. That's how to identify an Estate Planner.

When you consider evaluating an Estate Planner, you should look at the experience of the attorney, the wealth manager, and the CPA. At Nardulli & Associates, we are not "PRACTICING" on our clients.

We design Family Defined Benefit Plans. I have administered and managed coordination of hundreds of plans with our Elder Law Attorneys and CPA's since 1990.

What are your final thoughts for 55-75-year-olds who are considering estate planning and want to get their affairs in order?

The need for a Proper Estate plan is vital for the protection of yourself and your family for the correct succession of assets. Let's face it, it's inevitable - we don't live forever. Yet so many of us procrastinate when it comes to getting this aspect of our lives in order. A few years ago, I got sick and was out of work for a long time. At that time is when my wife and I realized in a personal way how important it is to have a proper Estate Plan in place before there's a need. That is also when I realized how the team approach in Estate Planning would protect clients. Our clients were well cared for during that time.

Now, when I meet with a potential client and they chose not to proceed with an Estate Plan, I worry about them and their family. I ask myself if there was anything I could have done or said differently that would have helped them to understand the importance of Estate Planning for their own sake and for their family. At Nardulli & Associates, I continually encourage and educate people in the hope that our message will inspire them to move forward with the protection of a proper working Estate Plan.

If someone feels they want to create estate plans for their families so they can have certainty, reduction of risk and feel comfortable in getting their affairs in order, how can they connect with you?

We always have an Estate Planning Workshop coming up. At these no-cost events, you will be able to meet me, our Elder Law Attorney, and other team members in person. It's the first step in your personal education on Estate Planning. The evening is mostly question led from the participants. You'll find that most people are experiencing the same confusion and feelings that you are.

At the workshop, you can schedule a free one-hour private meeting at our office, where you will have the opportunity to address your personal concerns and questions. We'll have a conversation to help you identify your Estate goals and dreams. If you are in need of a second opinion on your current Estate Planning documents, our Elder Law Attorney will provide a free review.

Check our website http://www.nardulliandassociates.com for upcoming dates. Or call us directly – we'd love to hear from you. (800) 969-7925 X200. Please feel free to check out our website for videos and articles on Estate Planning.

If you feel you're facing a problem that needs to be addressed right away, call my office and we will schedule a free one-hour meeting just as soon as we can. (800) 969-7925 X200

STEPHEN D. DISSETTE

Investment Advisor Representative
Horter Investment Management, LLC
Stephen D. Dissette & Associates

Email: sdissette@mindspring.com
Website: www.stephenddissetteandassociates.com
LinkedIn: https://linkedin.com/in/stephen-dissette
Cell: (630) 291-0904

Stephen Dissette is a graduate of Northwestern University. Upon graduation, he served as an officer in the United States Navy. He has 10 years of experience at an executive level in corporate America. Currently, he is a fiduciary with over 20 years of experience in the financial services industry and in addition, teaches a Retirement class for baby boomers at the college level.

As a young boy, he watched his grandfather work until final days unable to retire. His father also had to work into his 70s. This personal experience ignited his passion and desire to help pre-retirees and retirees through their retirement.

His mission is to help clients protect, preserve, and pass on their wealth to their families through a system designed to be low risk, low volatility and offer tax advantaged programs.

Your investment advisor may recommend third-party money managers who utilize investment strategies designed to minimize portfolio volatility and reduce the risk of declines in account values. Low Risk or Low Volatility strategies are generally defined as strategies that have a 10-year maximum drawdown of less than 10%. Like any other investment strategy, this approach entails risks, including the risk that client accounts can still lose value and the risk that a defensive position may, at any given point in time, prevent client accounts from appreciating in value.

STRIVING TO EXPERIENCE AND ENJOY
A WORRY-FREE RETIREMENT
By Stephen D. Dissette

Tell us about Stephen D. Dissette & Associates, the Retirees and Pre-retirees with and the types of situations they find themselves in when they come to you for your help?

My goal is to help Retirees and Pre Retirees protect, preserve, grow, and pass on their financial wealth, so they can have a long-lasting retirement, without running out of money. Additionally, my goal is to be an advisor people come to, to seek advice from and be someone they can trust and know I am working in their best interest. Some people have fear and concern they are not properly prepared for retirement. They are worried that they don't have enough money to both retire properly and have enough saved that they will not run out of their money during their retirement. There is so much confusion and fear in the world today with all the volatility and uncertainty.

One of my main objectives is that I want to help people establish and maintain a sense of peace of mind with their investment portfolio. Many people want to make sure their money is invested properly, in the right type of programs and with a much lower risk profile then what they currently have. The internet is at our fingertips today, which can be both a positive and a negative thing. There is almost too much information available, much of which is inaccurate. What sources do we believe? Most importantly, the question to ask is, in today's world, where can people find someone they can trust with their hard-earned retirement dollars?

What are the advantages of potentially protecting, preserving, growing, and passing on their financial wealth for Retirees and Pre-retirees?

There are four primary risks or threats to retirement. The first risk is taxes. Many Americans pay more than their fair share of taxes and there are many tax-advantaged programs available today that people are not aware of or do not know how to effectively utilize them. The second primary threat of retirement is long-term care. Even people that have built a large nest egg can have that crumble when addressing long-term care costs. The third risk to retirement is market risk with the possibility of losing a significant part of their nest egg. Lastly, longevity can be a major concern during retirement. Americans are living significantly longer than previous generations and this expanded life expectancy requires a much larger amount of money and can subject us to greater risks over time.

Having a plan or strategy in place to help protect a nest egg during retirement will allow people to have a long, successful, enjoyable and secure retirement. Ultimately, having a goal to protect and secure our wealth during retirement will allow us to create a legacy by effectively passing more of our wealth on to our families, beneficiaries and/or other charitable organizations.

What do you feel are the biggest myths out there when it comes to passing on financial wealth?

One of the biggest myths out there today is that someone can invest in a passive buy and hold philosophy in the stock market, still maintain their wealth, and ultimately pass that wealth on to the next generation. There are a couple common phrases that brokers and advisors will often tell their clients when the stock market is dropping. One of the expressions is, "don't worry it's only a paper loss." That is a completely false statement. If you need retirement funds and your account has dropped due to stock market losses, that is an actual loss of your wealth.

Another one of the classic lines that you will hear is, "oh don't worry you're in it for the long haul." At the point in someone's life when they are nearing retirement or already retired, are they really in it for the long haul? Take a look at the stock market performance from a high in March of 2000, followed by a 50% drop during the first downturn. This was followed by a market return, breaking even around 2008. A second major downturn of over 50% occurred during the financial crisis and then the market recovered, breaking even around 2012. What sort of a time-frame is that? A 12-year period is certainly not something that someone who is retired or nearing retirement can sustain with their wealth.

What are some common misconceptions around the Financial industry?

One of the biggest misconceptions in the investment world is there is a perfect answer for everyone. There is no cookie-cutter approach. Everyone's situation is different and unique. A person's risk tolerance must be considered. There is no one-size-fits-all. Everyone's individual needs and concerns must be addressed so they can strive to maintain and preserve their nest egg during retirement and to ultimately pass it on to the next generation.

Another misconception about the financial industry is that every broker or every advisor is looking out for your best interest. This may not always be the case. It is imperative that you work with someone who is a fiduciary. A fiduciary has as a legal standard that must be upheld. A fiduciary may only recommend something to you if it's in your best interest. Some brokers or advisors out there may only recommend what they consider a suitable investment to you. In some cases these investments are not always in someone's best interest.

Have a team of professionals assembled who will work to represent your best interests. A CPA, estate planning or Elder Law attorney, a social security expert, an investment professional, and an expert in health and long-term care planning are so important in planning for and navigating through retirement.

What are some of your client's most common fears around potentially protecting, preserving, growing, and passing on their financial wealth?

The biggest fear that pre-retirees have is whether they have enough money available to successfully retire, and is their money successfully invested. The biggest fear of retirees, once they are in retirement, is running out of money. People are concerned about health care costs that in today's retirement can run over a quarter million dollars during the retirement years. Long-term care costs of upwards of a six-figure cost per year, can wipe out even a large nest egg if needed for an extended period of time. Medical and health care costs are a legitimate concern during today's longer retirement years. No one wants to end up in a nursing home where their assets are utilized to cover long-term care expenses. As a last resort, the governmental program Medicaid kicks in. Retirees are very concerned about having to rely on the government as a last resort to fund extended long-term care costs, depleting the resources and leaving little or nothing to pass on to their family.

Market risk, global uncertainty and volatility of the investment markets are also a major concern and fear of investors in today's retirement world. This reminds me of a story about a gentleman who was turning age 65. He was ready to retire at that age in that year, and he had his entire retirement portfolio in his 401k at work. It was primarily invested in equity driven securities. In this gentleman's case, his portfolio dropped approximately 50%. His 401k in essence became a 201k. The tragedy for this gentleman was that he had to work five more years until his portfolio came back to the level it was in 2008. He worked until age 70, not because he wanted to, but because he had to. Just imagine how he felt.

The good news is that there are products and strategies that could potentially address these fears and concerns. Working with a financial professional will help you with your goals and needs of retirement.

How can Retirees and Pre-retirees get past those fears?

There is a very simple answer for pre-retirees as to when they can retire. They must have a plan to have enough income versus their expenses to provide the lifestyle they want and deserve in retirement. Retirement is all about lifestyle and lifestyle is driven by income. A person must have an income plan to prepare successfully for retirement. Sources of income during retirement include retirement savings plans such as 401k's, 403b's, 457 plans and IRAs, individual retirement arrangements.

Other sources of income may include a pension if available, social security and personal savings. Very important decisions need to be made if someone has a pension available. They may have an option to take a lump-sum distribution and roll into an IRA or to take a monthly pension payout. In addition, there are options for choosing a pension payout. Many plans offer multiple options. Once a decision is made, it cannot be changed. It becomes irrevocable and may have a lifelong impact. Regarding social security, it is crucial to decide at what age and when someone should file for social security. Although someone can file as early as age 62 in most cases, this is not always necessarily the best strategy. Often by waiting until their full retirement age (FRA) or even deferring all the way to age 70 to maximize social security benefits, may be their best strategy. These are very important decisions that should not be taken lightly. The advice of a professional fiduciary in these areas is highly recommended.

Once someone has successfully retired, there is a financial product available that will help guarantee someone's income for life. This will allow an individual to overcome the fear of outliving their money. One of the products is an annuity. For example, a pension is an annuity. There are several different options and varieties of annuities. Some are much more favorable to retirees than others. Again it is imperative that someone seek the advice of a professional fiduciary to ensure that their portfolio will address the risk of outliving their resources and risks involved with an annuity.*

Insurance and annuity products are not sold through Horter Investment Management, LLC ("Horter). Horter does not endorse any annuity or insurance products, nor does it guaranty their performance. Owners of these products are subject to the terms and conditions of the policies and contracts of the issuing company's strength and claims-paying ability.

What other perceived obstacles do you see that might be preventing the Retirees and Pre-retirees you help from seeking the help of an Investment Advisor?

Pre-retirees and retirees need to seek the advice of a professional fiduciary. There is a lot of confusion and uncertainty as to what truly constitutes a fiduciary. Some brokers and advisors in today's world can both be registered with a broker dealer and an RIA firm and still act in the fiduciary capacity. Look for someone who is a true fiduciary.

I understand how very difficult this is for many people. There is a joke about talking to ten different economists about a problem. How many different answers will you get? The answer is ten, but I remember one gentleman telling me twelve as an answer. You get my point. I always recommend seeing things in writing. I've always been a believer in the concept of trust, but verify. Just look at the facts. If you can't find something in writing, I wouldn't accept that as true.

When it comes to potentially protecting, preserving, growing, and passing on their financial wealth, what are some of the common pitfalls and mistakes you see Retirees and Pre-retirees make?

There are five primary pitfalls that pre-retirees and retirees need to avoid to help with the retirement they desire.

The first is drawing Social Security benefits too early. In most cases, the earliest someone can draw Social Security benefits is at age 62. This, however, is not necessarily the best strategy. Too many people jump on the bandwagon at age 62 to draw Social Security and their benefit is reduced by 25%. In other words, at age 62 a retiree will only draw 75% of their full retirement age benefit.

Your full retirement age is based upon the year that you are born. By deferring Social Security benefits until your full retirement age, which is typically between the ages of 66 and 67, a much greater percentage of your retirement income will be provided by the government through Social Security.

This depends on someone's lifespan and longevity. The longer someone will live, the more beneficial deferment of social security income would be. In order to maximize Social Security benefits, a retiree can wait until age 70 to draw Social Security. This would allow the maximum Social Security benefit for the rest of your life. In the event of spouse's passing, the surviving spouse would be able to draw the higher of the two Social Security checks.

This can be beneficial in today's world, where in many cases, a female spouse or a wife, typically can outlive a husband for many years. Especially in many cases, the husband is older than his wife. In today's world, at least 70% of baby boomer women will outlive their husbands on average of 15 to 25 years. (source, chartingyourfinancialfuture.com) If the husband was a greater wage-earner, an additional benefit of deferring Social Security would be to provide greater lifetime income for his surviving spouse.

Another pitfall to avoid is having too much risk in your retirement portfolio.

Generally speaking, as someone gets closer to retirement or is in retirement, less and less of a person's portfolio should be in a high-risk stock market type situation. A good example of why someone needs to be aware of this is what happened in 2008. You may recall my previous story about the gentleman where his 401k portfolio was primarily invested in equity driven securities. He was 65 years old and was about to retire. Unfortunately his portfolio dropped approximately 50%. His 401k, in essence, became a 201k. The tragedy he faced was he had to work 5 more years until his portfolio came back to the level. It was in 2008. He ended up working to age 70, not because he wanted to, but because he had to!

There is nothing wrong with someone wanting to work in retirement. As long as you are working because you want to, not because you have to. For all the football fans who understand the Red Zone in football, the five years prior to retirement and the first five years of retirement are the "Retirement Red Zone." Individuals cannot afford to have significant losses during this period. Market declines prior to five years or after five years will not have as great an impact on someone's retirement.

The third major pitfall to avoid is not having a large enough percentage of your portfolio devoted to guaranteed predictable income for life such as fixed annuity options.

A good rule of thumb is to have enough guaranteed income for life that will allow someone to cover their basic fixed costs in retirement. One of the best ways to ensure that is to invest in an income annuity either before retirement or during retirement. This guarantees an income stream to cover expenses. This will allow you to invest the rest of your portfolio more aggressively to help overcome the threat of inflation or rising cost of living during retirement years.

The fourth major pitfall to avoid is withdrawing too much of your retirement wealth too early in retirement.

The general rule of thumb is to withdraw no more than 4% of your retirement nest egg in any given year. For example, a $100,000 portfolio would generate $4,000 of income. A $500,000 portfolio would generate $20,000 a year of income. A million dollar portfolio would generate $40,000 of income a year, two million, $80,000 etc. The problem with the generally accepted 4% rule is this rule was established in the 1990's when interest rates were much higher. In today's interest rate environment, it may be more appropriate to withdraw 3% of your portfolio on an ongoing annual basis. This an opportunity for another source of Lifetime income. An income annuity may provide guaranteed income for you and a spouse if appropriate, so that you will not run out of money in retirement.

The final major pitfall to avoid is not having a plan in place that will help protect and cover long-term care expenses that may occur during retirement.

Most Americans are self-insured when it comes to long-term care expenses. Most are not adequately prepared in case of a long-term care event. A typical nursing home cost in today's world can be $253 daily or over $92,000 annually. (source: Genworth Financial) If the growth rate were to increase at 5% per year, then one year in a nursing home would cost nearly $200,000 in 20 years and near $325,000 in 30 years. (source: Kiplinger)

No matter how well-prepared someone is for retirement, an unexpected long-term care cost can decimate a nest egg. There are plans and programs that can help assist someone if a long-term care event does occur during retirement. It is important to work with a long-term care specialist to prepare for and have a plan in place in case of long-term care event during retirement.

How can these pitfalls or mistakes be avoided?

These pitfalls to a successful retirement or mistakes can be possibly be avoided by working with a financial professional who is a fiduciary who has your best interest at heart. It is imperative to have a plan in place that will cover when and how to draw Social Security. Your fiduciary can assist you with how much risk is acceptable in your retirement portfolio. Additionally, your fiduciary can advise what sources of guaranteed income are needed for life, especially if there's a couple involved. Lastly, your fiduciary can determine what percentage of your retirement Nest Egg can be withdrawn on a monthly or annual basis. It is imperative to have a plan in place to cover possible long-term care expenses in the future.

As a boy growing up, I was a Boy Scout. The Boy Scout's motto, as well as the Girl Scout's motto, is "be prepared". Serving in the United States Navy as an officer on the Battleship USS Iowa, I learned it is essential to have a plan in place. In other words, plan your work and work your plan. Many Americans go into retirement without a plan and woefully unprepared for retirement. Many go into retirement with a hope and a prayer plan.

Retirees hope they are prepared and pray they will have a successful retirement. These are important, but it is also very important to have a plan in place that is prepared in conjunction with a financial professional. The professional should be a fiduciary who gets to know you as a person. They should work in your best interest to cover your needs, concerns and goals in order to have a successful, worry-free retirement.

Can you share how you help Retirees and Pre-retirees and explain potential financial obstacles to succeed in having a long-lasting retirement, without running out of money.

When I get together with a potential client, I really get to know them. I learn about their dreams and goals. I also learn about their fears and concerns. After establishing a relationship, I do a fact finder and ask them simple questions they know the answers to. I then review their portfolio items. Often, I see people with accounts spread out all over the place with no overall plan in place. This is an obstacle I attempt to help overcome. They may have items that I recommend keeping. If I have a recommendation, it will be in their best interest. I work together with people to develop a strategy to potentially reach their financial goals. Together we may be able to consolidate their investments. I often present plans to assist in potentially maximizing social security benefits. If an annuity is appropriate, it may provide guaranteed income so my clients will not run out of money in retirement. This plan assists in helping my clients with the retirement they desire.

What led you to become an Investment Advisor?

My own personal family experiences inspired me to become an investment advisor. My grandfather passed away at age 65 on his way to work one day. He never saw a single day of retirement in his life. I was just a boy at the time, and I loved my grandfather. This event had a dramatic impact on me.

Unfortunately, he a left very little for my grandmother, his wife, and she struggled financially for the remainder of her life. My father worked until age 70 before he retired. He worked not because he wanted to, but because he had to. These personal family experiences in life drive me to help people. One of my primary goals in life now is to serve people by helping them have a secure, long-lasting and enjoyable retirement.

What's the most important thing Retirees and Pre-retirees should consider when evaluating an Investment Advisor?

The are several important factors retirees and pre-retirees should consider when selecting or evaluating an investment advisor. First, a relationship should be established, where the advisor has an opportunity to get to know you. This relationship should be based on trust where the advisors understand your goals, dreams and aspirations as well as your concerns and fears. The financial relationship should not be product driven. An Investment advisor should be on your team as a coach, directing, guiding, and helping you. In short, someone who truly is a fiduciary looking out for your best interest.

What are your final thoughts for Retirees and Pre-retirees considering their options for a potentially long-lasting retirement, without running out of money?

For the first time in the history of mankind, we are part of a generation that is facing perhaps decades in retirement. We live in a world with a lot of uncertainty and volatility. Most importantly, who do we trust in today's world with our hard-earned retirement dollars?

The good news is that with a proper plan in place, and working with a true fiduciary, you can help overcome the possible threats or obstacles we may face in retirement, and enjoy a long prosperous successful worry-free retirement.

If someone feels they want to protect, preserve, grow, and pass on their financial wealth, so they can potentially have a long-lasting retirement, without running out of money, how can they connect with you and what will happen when they do?

If someone wants to reach out to and connect with me, they may do so through my website www.stephenddissetteandassociates.com. I can also be directly contacted by phone or via my email.

If it is appropriate, we will set a time to get together for a personal consultation. There is no cost, no obligation, or pressure of any sort during our consultation. You may ask as many questions as you would like and I will answer you with simple, easy to understand language and will show you in writing as well. I will review your current investments. If you have something that is good and appropriate for you, I will let you know. If I can offer you something that is more suitable, I will let you know as well. Remember, I am a fiduciary. I will only recommend something to you if it's in your best interest.

There are also opportunities if someone would like to consult with me, to attend either a retirement presentation conducted on a regular basis, or to attend one of my retirement classes taught at a local college.

I tell people I work in the financial industry, but that I am in the people business. I'm not sure if I can help you out or not, but I would welcome the opportunity to get together with you and see what I can do to help you in any way possible. Remember that you don't know what you don't know. Even if you are working with a current advisor, it makes a lot of sense for you to get a second professional opinion.

Don't miss out on the opportunity to have a long, successful retirement you desire. I look forward to hearing from you. God bless you and I wish you a successful voyage as you navigate throughout your entire retirement journey.

Investment advisory services offered through Horter Investment Management, LLC, an SEC-Registered Investment Advisor. Horter Investment Management does not provide legal or tax advice. Investment Advisor Representatives of

Horter Investment Management may only conduct business with residents of the states and jurisdictions in which they are properly registered or exempt from registration requirements. Insurance and annuity products are sold separately through Stephen D. Dissette & Associates. Securities transactions for Horter Investment Management clients are placed through TCA by E*TRADE, TD Ameritrade and Nationwide Advisory Solutions.

TRENT A. DRANSFIELD

Retirement Advisor & Life Coach

Dransfield & Associates

Email: drans007@netzero.com
Website: https://DransfieldAndAssociates.com
Call: (800) 364-1022

Trent Dransfield has been a recognized speaker, life coach, and Retirement Advisor for the past sixteen years. Prior to that, Trent received his Bachelor's degree at the University of Utah. Shortly thereafter, he pursued the medical field and graduated from Physical Therapy school. After school, he practiced as a professional clinician in a variety of settings with an emphasis in Orthopaedic Outpatient rehabilitation.

After practicing for five years, he set sail and began working part-time learning about Retirement planning and the field of finance. He was quite intrigued by how his retirement would pan out and began assisting others to learn the importance of becoming more educated and understanding their retirement plan.

Trent is currently the President of Dransfield & Associates where he runs three offices with a fabulous staff of six while allowing himself a balanced life approach of serving as a volunteer in his church and Physical Therapy.

He also takes time as a life coach for teenagers and adults, presenting to thousands on stage and assisting them to find their true potential and take on their dreams! He loves his family, his wonderful wife Andrea and seven children. He also enjoys the outdoors, fitness, composing music and living life to its fullest!

RETIRING, NOW WHAT?
By Trent A. Dransfield

Tell us about Dransfield & Associates, the people you work with and the types of situations they find themselves in when they come to you for your help?

I assist people in retirement to preserve and protect their legacy, so they can sleep well at night knowing their retirement money will never run out. Years ago, I really wasn't planning on leaving the medical field. It was stable, rewarding and enjoyable. However, when I found out in 2002 that we had lost 68% in our financial portfolio and not understanding what we were invested in, I began realizing that I knew nothing about finances and wondered if others were in that same boat.

So I took a part-time job learning more about finances, issuing CD's (certificates of deposit) and asking the retired population how their retirement was going. I was surprised to find that most clients did not have a true definitive road map and game plan for their retirement. Instead, it was more like "hoping for the best" or living in the mystery of retirement. I quickly realized this could be a big problem!

What I have created with all of my clients over the years is a thorough focus, on first and foremost, educating them on the fundamentals of retirement and the necessary steps of reaching what they desire. Have they maximized their Social Security, or minimized their taxes? Do they truly understand their accounts? What are their goals and passions in this life? Do they have a definite timeline laid out which shows they will never outlive their money?

I learned a valuable tool in the field of physical therapy... to objectively measure improvements while you treat the patient. Followed by constant ways of measuring improved results. This requires knowing what your goals are and implementing a set plan to achieve those goals while communicating with the patient on improvement. I believe these techniques (measuring, communicating and following protocols) can be used in the field of retirement. Just like a life preserver to hold us up in a storm, having a solid retirement plan can keep us afloat amidst the turbulent waves of financial upheavals that lie in wait.

What are the advantages of preserving and protecting their legacy?

Imagine walking into a room where you greet a friend and client, named Owen. He sits down sheepishly in the chair in front of your desk. His head down and shoulders hunched over in his chair staring at the ground. As you sit down at your desk across from Owen, you are wondering why he is carrying himself in this manner, just as if his body language is saying "my life is ruined, nothing but bad news for me."

As you look into his eyes you decide to ask the golden question... "Owen, tell me how things are going?" Owen slowly raises his head to make eye contact with yours and responds by saying: "Trent, you see, my wife and I have had these dreams...dreams for years of traveling to several beautiful destinations in Europe, walking through the downtown cobblestone streets of Norway, diverging to yet another trip to Ireland while taking in the coastal air and breathtaking views of the green rolly hills as we watch the sunset.

We picture ourselves traveling to some of the most glorious beaches, feeling the white sand in between our toes only to smile, realizing that we are living our dreams! You see, Trent, we have written an incredible bucket list for so many years and dreamt that one day we would do it all! We have waited our whole life to finally enjoy these exciting times! I remember with all of those long, hard working hours, day after day, that someday after retirement I would be living the life!

Trent, we finally got to our destination of retirement, and now, as we anxiously approached our broker a few days ago, he tells us this... "Owen, the bad news, you have lost nearly 55% of your portfolio for the past sixteen months, but don't worry, it will come back up." "Trent, I am getting older and so badly have wanted to take my sweetheart across the world and experience these awesome travels and now, to hear these words coming out of our broker's mouth, similar to someone rubbing salt in my wounds, I now realize I am not able to fulfill these amazing dreams because now... I can't afford them! I am speechless, devastated and don't know where to go or what to do."

After hearing real stories like this transpire, I realized I am driven in creating a solid plan for my clients that simply wipes out the ambiguous mystery of financial ups and downs! I can now create a measurable game changer that allows my clients the opportunity to attain their dreams while preserving and protecting their legacy! This is why I am passionate about what I do.

Doesn't every client deserve the opportunity to live their dreams? It's like hiking in a cave without a map and a flashlight... it's not going to get you too far! By having the necessary roadmap and plenty of lighting, it will make that destination pleasant, offering a for sure step by step walk through the luminous caverns of life. By preserving and protecting one's legacy with a well-constructed roadmap, the path is easily attainable getting you what you want!

What do you feel are the biggest myths out there when it comes to preserving and protecting their legacy?

Some of the biggest myths out there when it comes to preserving and protecting their legacy are people not fully understanding and being educated on their accounts for retirement. There can be an assumption that says something like this..." we think we are ok with our future." Really? If you don't fully understand your accounts and how they work then how will you know if they will be working for you? My point is this, you must identify what you want and then see if you have in your retirement arsenal items that will get you what you want.

It is important to get educated and really find out what you want and then go find that strategy to get what you want. Quit relying on someone else telling you what to do and you say "sure, whatever you say." Educating yourself can only improve the vision of your direction. The higher you climb the ladder, the more you can see around you. That's the same idea with gaining knowledge for your retirement. Keep learning and don't stop!

Here's another food for thought... you may have the most immaculate knee brace that will support a knee, but if the issue is swelling or inflammation in the elbow, what good is that knee brace? Know the underlying problem, then simply get the solution that addresses that issue.

What are some common misconceptions around the Finance industry?

Some of the basic misconceptions I see in the Finance industry are that by researching topics on the internet, one can find all of the solutions. In today's world, yes, it is more easily accessible and great information can be found, however, getting someone who has experience dealing with finances and deals with it on a daily basis for years can have some great tips and advice to offer you.

A second misconception I often see are those that feel like they have enough knowledge based upon their financial experience and choose to simply manage and take on their own retirement without continually seeking further education and professional advice. A survey by Charles Schwab found that one in three people don't seek any outside input when it comes to managing their money. Some people have a notion that getting financial advice is too expensive and it could cost more than they could afford. The reality? There are professionals that offer reasonable hourly or fixed-fees. Sitting down for a few hours can make a drastic change in your financial future!

A third misconception... "Hey, I've hired a financial advisor, now I don't need to do anything." That's where you can get into danger. Just like standing too close to the fire for a prolonged period of time... you may get some permanent scarring and get burned! Remember a good planner requires your input and you should be working and collaborating as a team to get to your destination!

What are some of your client's most common fears about creating dependable cash flow for their retirement?

My clients' most common fears about cash flow for their retirement is simply this ... is it really attainable? Some believe as a fixed belief that money or the process of investing has to look a certain way. Have you ever thought of this? If you need to cross the room from point A to point B and you have thirty people all with the same intention of moving from one side to the other, can they do it even if they are instructed that they cannot mimic one other person in the group? Absolutely. It doesn't have to look a certain way. There are several ways that can work to create a dependable cash flow for their retirement and we love teaching these techniques that simply work!

Another fear I commonly hear that is a real beast out there in the wild is "will I run out of my money?" The number one fear and problem in the retired sector is truly outliving one's money. What would your life look like if you knew exactly how much you will be receiving month to month and knowing when to turn on another spigot of money to hold you over and deal with the heavyweight fighter called taxes and inflation?

Picture yourself in front of a drawn-out timeline on the whiteboard. You can see clearly your different income buckets you can count on and when times get tough or inflation and taxes start hitting you on the head, you can easily and appropriately turn additional income on to sustain the blows! Wow, what a concept.

Keep in mind, you can choose to live the life of mystery wondering when your money will outlive your lifestyle and thus run out of money or have an "autopilot" plan that allows you the necessities in life while pursuing what you really want to do... enjoying your time and capturing the moments of life!

Another fear I hear from my clients is not wanting to change or explore new arenas that sound good and can alter their financial future for a road protected and safe yet "less traveled" because they are used to the norm of doing what they were told to do for years and years. I have heard of clients that realize the roadmap they now have may be one with risk and they say to me, "I can't afford to lose any more of my hard earned money", yet are hesitant to change for fear of ruining a relationship with their broker or brokerage firm. (Yes, even after they admit to having lost nearly one million dollars from the scarring effects of the past volatile market).

How can people in retirement get past those fears?

People in retirement can get past these fears by simply gaining more education, finding out what type of accounts you actually own and doing some good ole' research. Then tune into what you want. What percent are you willing to lose or have at risk? Are your accounts at risk? The more detailed you get at finding what you want, you will have a clearer picture of seeing if your accounts are lining up with your desires.

If they are, then congratulations, you are on your way. If not, get excited to jump into the unknown and set a new course to sail! It could lead you in a direction that makes more sense to you! Get excited about learning more about your retirement. The more you learn, the higher your confidence will rise and you can make more choice decisions to impact you and your legacy!

Remember to start using strategies in finances that will give you those sound guarantees and provisions to allow you a dependable cash flow so you can focus on doing the things you love to do! Use proven techniques and strategies that will get you a roadmap that does not deviate or create uncertain paths that can lead you off the path! This is where you deserve to have a concrete well laid out game plan that you can count on no matter what!

Finally, do what is best for you. This is your hard earned money and you deserve to know how to best utilize this to sustain a continuous path of dependable cash flow. Don't always simply agree and do what the savvy advisor tells you to do. Learn from them yet do your own homework as well!

What other perceived obstacles do you see that might be preventing people in retirement from seeking the help of a Retirement Advisor?

People often may feel that seeking the help of a Retirement Advisor "costs too much." Like I previously mentioned, they can offer reasonable fee based or hourly fees and their advice may save you thousands down the road. Another obstacle may be that you have had a bad experience in the past and thus, a challenge to seek further professional advice. Ask around and get someone who can trust that feels knowledgeable yet truly hears what you want for your retirement!

When it comes to preserving and protecting their legacy, what are some of the common pitfalls and mistakes you see people in retirement make?

Some of the pitfalls I see people make are simply trusting their advisor to make all the decisions and not taking the necessary steps in further educating themselves. This can provide new insight, validation of how your plan is working and in alignment or not. Then you will feel more confident in changing the course to better fit your situation. Other pitfalls to watch out for in the industry can be hidden fees buried in the small print of contracts.

If you call your brokerage firm and you hear that you aren't being charged any fees, then get it in writing. In most cases, there are hidden fees there. Also look for professionals that have been established with great years of experience. Unqualified professionals with attractive low fees can sometimes look exciting but beware and do your homework.

How can these pitfalls or mistakes be avoided?

You can avoid these pitfalls by doing your homework. Research and get more educated on products and the companies with whom you choose to work. Make sure you get everything in writing. Nowadays, simply by hearing someone tell you a certain thing, it's not like the good ole' handshake in days of old. Get everything in writing. You want to find out all of your fees, including those that are in hiding!

Share an example of how you have helped someone to overcome those obstacles and succeed in gaining peace of mind knowing their retirement money will never run out.

For example, I had a gentleman come in stating that his retirement was "good." I asked him what that meant, and if he understood his accounts to which he responded with "kind of." I then recommended that he begin dissecting his accounts and asking himself what the purpose of each account was for. As he began digging in with questioning his accounts he realized that most of his money was not where he wanted them at this point in his life. By taking the time to further analyze and find out what he really wanted, we were able to achieve it with enough questions, homework and time.

Here's food for thought… literally.

Picture you walking into the Convenient store. You walk up to the cashier and say "give me something good to eat" to which he reaches down and gives you a chocolate donut! So you pound it and later feel like crap! You do some research and find out that you could have ordered a healthy green protein smoothie! Well, you do the education, then you will know what you want. The same goes true with this example.

The gentleman didn't really know what was "good" and once he was properly educated, he started making decisions that were a good fit for him.

What led you to become a Retirement Advisor & Life Coach?

Wow, what a great question. I was treating patients in Physical therapy and one day noticed my prospectus statement lying on the table. "What is that on the table? ... oh yeah, that's one of those hundred page papers bound together that killed a few trees and I don't understand one lick of it. It was like studying a foreign language. But some gut feeling made me begin reading it.

It wasn't until about page 93 where I found certain fees and that I had lost nearly 70% of my portfolio from the past eighteen months! Now that grabbed my attention. So, I started picking up books about finances and retirement as a hobby.

Yep, a hobby!

Then I found myself wanting to see if anyone else could relate. Next thing I knew, I was working part-time assisting in retirement planning and the rest is history! Now I assist people in retirement planning full time and have been doing that straight sixteen years!!! Go figure. Oh yea, and I love what I do!

What's the most important thing people in retirement should consider when evaluating a Retirement Advisor?

First and foremost find out what their intention is and more about them as a person.

Are they in it for their pocketbook or for your real interest? Ask them why they decided to do what they do. Listen and get a gut feeling about that individual.

Sometimes you have to swim through all of the credentials to really see if this is a person you can trust and really connect with let alone learn valuable tools!

What are your final thoughts for people in retirement who want to be sure their retirement money never runs out?

My final thoughts are this…

Have them really get a deeper understanding of what their accounts are doing, and how they work and then decide if that is where they want the money. Then use the necessary safe vehicles in retirement that can truly give them a guaranteed lifetime payout they can always count on so they can sleep at night and spend their time doing the things they have dreamt of instead of fretting around a computer screen or television trying to figure out what to do.

If someone feels they want to preserve and protect their legacy, so they can sleep well at night knowing their retirement money will never run out, how can they connect with you?

I have a free report about not outliving your hard earned money on my website at www.dransfieldandassociates.com On page 18 there is a special code only for readers of this book chapter. Quote that code in email to drans007@netzero.com or phone calls to us and you will receive a free report that will give you a step by step bulletproof plan to overcome the risks of outliving your money and creating peace of mind to always have sufficient money for all of your retirement.

If you feel like you are facing this similar problem of outliving or not fully understanding your retirement, the best thing you can do is give me a call at (800) 364-1022 and we will walk you through step by step a simple way to get you back on your feet and in the right direction!

GARY R. WAITZMAN, JD/CPA

Licensed Producer
Gary R. Waitzman Strategies
Law Offices of Gary R. Waitzman, LLC

Email: gary@grweplaw.com
Website: http://www.grweplaw.com
LinkedIn: https://www.linkedin.com/in/garywaitzman25
Facebook: https://www.facebook.com/LawOfficesofGRW
Twitter: https://twitter.com/LawOfficesofGRW
Call: (847) 719-1300 | **Direct Number:** (847) 793-9103

Gary R. Waitzman is founder of the Law Offices of Gary R. Waitzman, LLC and Gary R. Waitzman Strategies in Lincolnshire, Illinois. His practice focuses on wealth management, estate planning, asset protection and legacy planning.

Gary graduated from the University of Illinois in 1973 and earned his CPA license in 1975 and his J.D. from John Marshall Law School in 1979.

Mr. Waitzman spent 10 years at a regional public accounting firm and 19 years as managing partner of a 40 attorney law firm.

Mr. Waitzman is a member of the National Academy of Elder Law Attorneys (NAELA), Wealth Counsel (a National Network of Estate Planning Attorney's), American Association of Attorney-Certified Public Accountants (AAA-CPA), Illinois State Bar Association, The American Bar Association, Illinois State Certified Public Accountants, American Institute of Certified Public Accountants, and a member of the MPS Organization.

Gary lives in Riverwoods, IL with his wife Katie, Buster, the wonder dog, and Cubby, a second dog member of our family. He is close with his children and six grandchildren; Alyssa, Brayden, Jase, Kayla, Carli, and Morgan.

RETIRING? HOW DO WE MAKE IT WORK AND STOP THE BLEEDING?

By Gary R. Waitzman

Tell us about Gary R. Waitzman Strategies, the individuals you work with and the types of situations they find themselves in when they come to you for your help?

My goal is to become your most trusted advisor.

I help individuals 58 and older who are nearing retirement or retired to reduce risk with their wealth, so they can recognize the impact market volatility can have on their retirement and help them avoid that disastrous result.

I do this by working with the clients to identify their biggest concerns, the ones keeping them up at night and prioritizing how we are going to solve these issues one at a time.

I frequently sit down with people that have varied investments and they have little grasp of how much at risk they truly are. This is both in the overlapping of similar investments as well as the overall amount of their wealth that is subject to market risk.

In the volatile market that we are now in this is a recipe for disaster with our retirement plans. What we hoped would work suddenly seems to be going in the completely wrong direction. Plans that fail once we are close to retiring is one of the biggest fears of the people when I first meet them. Making sure those bad results don't happen is what I am most passionate about helping my clients accomplish.

What are the advantages of reducing investment risk for your clients?

I continue to see people in their 60's and 70's who are afraid of missing out on the wonderful increases in the markets of the last nine years or so. As a result, they are extremely over investing in risk-oriented strategies, i.e. stocks, bonds, mutual funds, ETFs, and others. People love to tell me that they feel safe because they are spreading their risk by diversifying into less risky investments. My job is to educate them about the fact that taking less risk is not the same as eliminating the risk altogether.

The main advantage of this approach is locking in gains already made and not giving them back to the market once they have been earned. My approach is to help my clients determine what amount of risk, if any, is appropriate to take depending on their goals, objectives, age and net worth. Then find approaches for them to move forward with reduction or elimination of risk completely. We make sure they will never lose their money and keep their money as free from risk as they need and want. This helps my clients to make sure they will never run out of money in their retirement years.

What do you feel are the biggest myths out there when it comes to reducing investment risk?

For me, the biggest myth is that as the markets start downward movements (as they are mostly doing now and I expect to see this continue) that my clients should not worry. How often do I hear other advisors saying, "it's a paper loss" "you're in it for the long haul" "don't worry, markets always come back". While some of this may be true, the reality is that as we age, we have less and less time to recover new losses as we approach retirement or may already be retired. What made sense when we were investing in our 30's or 40's or even our 50's makes less and less sense as we age. Why, you may ask?

We have less and less time until we need to start using some of these funds and a much shorter time horizon with which to recover our losses yet again. Many of us lived thru 2001 and 2008. While most of us did recover our losses from those bad markets, it took many years to do so.

If we experience the same 40 or 45 percent drop as we did then, we most likely will never fully recover. In addition, as we need to access our funds to finance our retirement lifestyle they are no longer available to recover new gains to offset the loss that has taken place. All these issues factor into misleading my clients into believing the myth that taking losses due to excessive risky investments really don't matter. THEY DO!

What are some common misconceptions about the Legal or Financial Services industries?

The biggest misconception I see today is that the Financial Advisors being "fiduciaries" somehow gives the public better protections than what previously existed. As an Attorney and

CPA, I have been held to Fiduciary standards for over thirty years. It basically means that the Legal or Financial Services professional is expected to put the best interest of the client ahead of their own. I have worked in this way my entire professional career and the DOL rule changes nothing in terms of how I work and protect my clients.

The better question is "why haven't all the professionals out there been putting their clients' interests first ALWAYS? Why did the DOL have to create a rule to make these people protect their clients. This is the classic case of Buyer Beware. If your Lawyer or Financial Services professional does not follow this rule, they should not be practicing in the first place. If you have any doubts about where your professional is coming from, it's time to find a new Lawyer or Financial Advisor.

I pride myself on full transparency and communication with my clients so that they know my number one passion is protecting and helping them accomplish their objectives and feel really good about Legal and Financial decisions they are making with my help.

What are some of the most common fears about their retirement?

The most common fear I see in meeting with people is the fear of not having enough money to live the way they hope to live in retirement. People plan and scrimp and save for years in order to live the dream life after they retire. What I hear over and over is do I have enough assets to live to my life expectancy without sacrificing my lifestyle goals or simply will I run out of money once I retire? There are many different options and approaches available to make sure we can deal with these fears and meet my clients' goals.

However, just like any other life-changing decision, the client must be ready to make the choices and follow thru in order to implement my suggestions and address their fears. I frequently deal with the client fighting with their conflict of being afraid of having enough money but also being scared to make important changes to help solve the problem. I spend much of my time helping the client come to grips with this important choice that they must make.

Otherwise, as the saying goes, "if you keep doing what you've been doing, you'll keep getting what you've been getting." This includes the biggest fear of basically failing to live the life they want in retirement.

How can individuals who are nearing retirement or retired get past those fears?

As I said, people have to be ready to have a serious conversation with me. I don't do high pressure anything. I simply educate my clients with the hope that they let me help them. Sometimes they do and sometimes they don't. I always encourage people to watch the videos on my website to try and get to know me a little better, so they are more comfortable when we get to the down and dirty about what needs to happen to solve the cause of their fears.

Once I have the chance to review the client's' information and objectives my work really begins. How can I best describe the options to the client and help them see that even though it is something new and different from how they may be doing it right now, in the long run, my suggestion will help take them thru their retirement in the lifestyle they so desire.

People have to prepare themselves to make those changes that are necessary. Making no decision is a decision. If they fail to plan, they plan to fail. My biggest hope and goal is to help them make a better choice.

What other perceived obstacles do you see that might be preventing the individuals you work with from seeking the help of an Estate Planning Attorney or Financial Advisor?

I actually think about this all the time. Why? Why won't people listen? Why do they resist following my advice? Sometimes the solution seems so clear to me. How can I say it better? How can I educate my clients better? I want to help the whole world and it can be very frustrating for me as the Professional that people decide to keep things as they are and not take my help.

I believe that many people have had so many bad experiences where someone tried to take advantage of them that they become cynical and unwilling to let anyone help them. In some cases, it may just be bad luck or timing that they have met with the wrong people.

Often people come to see me, and they have read articles or watched shows or heard interviews on the radio or whatever and as a result of this information, they don't think I can help them.

Usually, when I have the chance to drill down with them a bit, I can point out that they are taking some of the information out of context or perhaps not fully understanding what the other people were saying.

In any case, my clients may have heard what they needed to hear to convince themselves that leaving everything alone is the best course of action. I pride myself in the fact that I will not make a suggestion unless and until I know that I am helping the person sitting in front of me.

Whether the issue is an Estate Planning issue or a Financial Services issue, I am going to do my best to help the person be in a better position than they were when they first come to visit me.

What are some of the little-known pitfalls and common mistakes you see people making with their investments?

The biggest mistake I see all too often is people having way too much of their wealth invested in assets subject to market risk. I had one person in the workshops I present raise his hand when I reviewed the chart of the historical movements in the S&P 500 Stock index. I then asked who believed the stock market would continue to rise in spite of the most current 9 ½ year Bull run we have just gone thru.

Everyone but him agrees the market is due for a very significant decline in value in the near term future. In spite of almost universal agreement about the impending downturn, people are reluctant to change their strategy as to how much of their money should be at risk in the markets.

Usually, this is because they are not sure if the market has topped out or not. I try to point out that they may be risking an unlikely additional upside of perhaps five percent against the much more likely result of a thirty or forty percent decline.

I ask my clients to imagine a thirty or forty percent drop in value and imagine the impact that would have on their retirement assets. In my opinion, peace of mind will only happen by the client deciding to reduce the amount of risk they are currently exposed to.

This is clearly an area that I can and want to help my clients with. Once again, the most important issue is whether the client is ready to make a change or simply thinking about it. I ask people to please not give in to analysis paralysis.

While they are thinking the market may be tanking and they could be losing the very assets that they are depending on to help them thru retirement.

How can these pitfalls or mistakes be avoided?

After we meet, and I have a chance to review the personal situation of my client, if I can help the person to be in a better position by eliminating some of the risks they have taken I make a recommendation to them. Typically I suggest moving some of their money into a safe money alternative. This may be one of the hundreds of different possibilities, but I select and suggest what I believe will be most helpful for their particular situation. It must be what I feel is in their best interest.

After our review and thorough explanation of the suggested option, it is up to the client to make a final decision about whether they are ready to move forward. When they are it is my job to implement the strategy for my client and stay in constant communication with them until it is in place. The client is always in charge of this process. My job is to educate to motivate them in order to allow me the chance to help them safeguard their futures.

Share an example of how you have helped someone to overcome these obstacles and succeed in obtaining peace of mind during retirement?

I met with a couple two years ago who were considering near-term retirement. They were concerned that significant market drops could be a straw that would break the camel's back as far as being able to go thru with their retirement plan.

I reviewed several possible ideas I had for them which completely eliminated any possible risk from market losses. After thorough discussions and explanations, they decided on a wonderful option that gave them total peace of mind. They are now enjoying their dreams worry-free as young retired baby boomers.

In another case, a 75-year-old lady who had already retired was working with a large brokerage firm. She had not heard from anyone at this firm for over three years. In the meantime, she was heavily invested in stocks and mutual funds which were actually losing value in a very good market.

She didn't know what to do to address this. She was introduced to me and after a thorough review of her situation, I made a suggestion that dramatically reduced her market risk. She agreed with my safe money alternative suggestion and we moved a significant amount of her money.

She is now very happy and the investments she had been in before would have cost her significantly more losses if she had not agreed to make the move. It was very gratifying to me to see how much I was able to help this lady.

What inspired you to become an Estate Planning Attorney and Financial Advisor?

Since I was very young I had wanted to be an Attorney. I first became a CPA after college but never gave up my dream. After I passed the CPA exam I started night law school four evenings a week for four years. I passed the Bar exam and eventually opened my first law office. I always enjoyed helping my clients save taxes and so I found myself helping more and more families reduce their taxes and passing the family wealth from generation to generation in the most efficient and cost-effective ways possible.

As time passed I became more and more aware of situations where clients were being taken advantage of and led down very poor paths in their investing strategies. I became aware of many advisors who were actually acting in their own commissions' best interest, not their clients'. I decided with my abilities as an Attorney and CPA that I could help steer these people in a safer course with the financial background I had acquired thru years of professional practice in different areas.

I got my license in the financial services area and am now able to assist my clients in many ways depending on their individual needs and concerns. I love helping my clients with my multidisciplinary abilities.

What's the most important consideration when retaining an Estate Planning Attorney or Financial Advisor?

In my opinion, the most important consideration in retaining an Attorney or Financial Advisor is the level of trust and likability of the advisor that the client is considering. Trust is important because the client needs to know that the

Professional is on their side and advising them in a way that is in the clients' best interest.

The client has to feel that any suggestion is what is best for them and they believe this with all their heart. As one client recently put it, this is the biggest financial decision they had ever made in their lives and how scary that was. How can we as Professionals expect someone to allow us to help them if they don't completely trust us?

Likability is also extremely important because I believe to do a thorough job, my relationship with the client has to make the client comfortable to meet with me on a continuing basis. I have a relationship based practice and I educate my clients that we will be working together for years to come and I expect to meet with every one of them at least annually. How can that happen if we don't truly like each other?

Trust and likability are the keys to a mutually wonderful and beneficial relationship.

What are your final thoughts for individuals 58 and up who are nearing retirement or retired and recognize the impact market volatility can have on their retirement?

In 2008 and 2009 I personally lost 45% of my retirement assets. It was an awful and sobering experience. The good news is that I was young enough to recover much of what I lost. But what if the same thing is happening right now and I am ten years older than the last market downturn? Do I have enough time left to wait for the markets to be kind enough to let me recover what I lost?

WHY GIVE BACK THE GAINS FROM THE LAST 9 ½ YEARS TO THE MARKET?

We have a golden opportunity right now to make sure the bleeding of our assets does not make us unable to comfortably live thru our retirement years without having to work again or seriously cut back on the lifestyle we had hoped to enjoy. We can seriously consider moving enough of our assets to safe money alternatives right now before we are hit with serious losses that affect us for the rest of our lives.

Please let me help you right now to avoid the horrible potential consequences of a market drop of 30 or 40 or 45%. You have the power right now, but the window will not last indefinitely. Some people choose to go it on their own and not work with me. Repeatedly, I visit with them at a later time and they have done a great deal of damage which could have been avoided if they had worked with me in the first place. Why wait?

If anyone nearing retirement or retired wants to reduce risk on their investments in order to minimize the potential impact of market volatility, how can they get in touch with you?

I do workshops every month talking about many of the topics I have discussed in this chapter. For an invitation to one of my dinner workshops, please contact my office at (847)

719-1300 or (847) 793-9103 and we will help you with a registration to our next available workshop. We will take some basic information from you and make sure you get registered to a mutually convenient date and time.

You can also email me at gwaitzman@grweplaw.com and we will get you registered if that is more convenient. We strive to make the process of working with us as simple as possible. At the workshop, you will be given the opportunity to have an initial no-fee no-cost consultation with me about any of the issues we discuss.

I am a multi-faceted Professional and this truly is an opportunity you will not have in our area. Of 1000 other advisors in my area, I am the only Attorney/CPA/Financial Professional around. If you have major medical concerns do you visit with a General Practitioner or do you go see the Specialist who may save your life? In this arena, I am the "Specialist". Please take advantage of this opportunity and let me help you.

My specific "Call to Action" is this, please contact me using any of the above suggestions for an initial complimentary consultation.

When you contact us, we will walk you through specifically what information is needed for me to have the most productive consultation with you and help us get to the serious issues which may be keeping you up at night. The sooner we do this, the sooner you will benefit from this opportunity.

PHILLIP M. SCHEIBER, FICF

Scheiber & Associates Financial

Email: pscheiber@srins.com
Website: http://www.srins.com
LinkedIn: https://Linkedin.com/in/PhillipScheiber
Facebook: S&A InsuranceServices
Call: (952) 649-0504 | **Call:** (800) 327-2145

Phil is an expert in the areas of retirement planning, business continuation planning, retirement plan solutions for businesses and individuals, asset protection, estate planning and Medicare health plans.

He has received numerous awards from both Fraternal and Stock Companies. His awards have been for service and customer satisfaction. He has been recognized by the Knights of Columbus by being awarded the coveted "Supreme Knights' Club" award five times, and by earning awards from Brokers' International, Million Dollar Round Table, 'Eagle Forum' and from the Better Business Bureau. He has been heard on KCHK radio, as well as AM 1330 Relevant Radio.

Having taught finance and financial management at no fewer than two institutions of higher education, he is well known as a teacher, coach, and leader. As an experienced advocate for his clients, he provides detailed and personal research for each of his clients. Hs is known for his thoroughness and providing the best solutions to meet his clients' needs.

Phil is definitely someone you want to have advising you in your financial and estate issues, so that in retirement, or a crisis you have peace of mind.

A PRIMER ON ASSET PROTECTION
By Phillip M. Scheiber

Tell us about Scheiber & Associates Finance and how you are helping your clients?

I help people who are nearing retirement or in retirement to preserve their assets so they can have guaranteed income for life, feel secure and enjoy peace of mind in their retirement.

The chief concern of most people in retirement or preparing for retirement is, "Will I run out of money in retirement?"

There are other concerns, but this is the focal point that includes issues of, "What if I get sick and need care?", "What happens if my spouse gets sick and needs care?", and, "Can I maintain my lifestyle?"

All of these stem from the anxiety of 'running out of money'. The issue behind 'running out of money is the preservation of assets. This problem is not age-related. If someone is in retirement or nearing retirement there is the anxiety and fear related to (1) "Will my assets last for the rest of my life" and (2) "Will my assets preserve my standard of living?" My job is to distill the information they give me. Then I can match their assets to their stated goals, making it simple. This gives the client the confidence to move ahead.

If someone is not near retirement, their anxieties will be based on the same concerns; but with the added facet of accumulation to the concern for protection. In this case, I help clients focus on saving and the protection of income against unforeseen events such as disability or premature death.

The most important thing I do is focus on preserving their assets, whether those assets are real estate, investments, income assets, pensions, or their current income and obligations.

What are the advantages of preserving assets for people who are nearing retirement or in retirement?

Imagine you are on a boat leaving a harbor. You don't know how long the trip will last, but you know approximately how much distance is between you and a distant harbor. You have checked your fuel, provisions, mechanical systems, and navigational equipment. You figure you can go 25 knots, and get there with plenty of everything to spare.

You got a for a while. Everything is going to plan. Fuel is plentiful. A few days in you get a headwind and a chop. You are too far out to turn back. You reduce speed. The wind picks up some more. You reduce speed again to conserve fuel. Meanwhile, water and food run short. You didn't plan on rough weather.

The fuel gauge is running ever lower as you try to make the still distant destination. What had seemed like an easy cruise is now turned into an inconvenience, if not a life-threatening situation. Running out of fuel means everything stops. Each time you reduce speed to conserve fuel you have to shut down air conditioning, refrigeration. lights, navigational equipment, etc. The entire passengers and crew are now frightened.

Retirement is much like the story above. In many cases, retirees believe the stock market and the stock market alone is the key to their successful retirement. They go off into retirement without a distinct plan to ensure there is enough 'fuel' and the right 'speed' to get through their retirement without having to make major adjustments.

I assist clients in defining how to position assets so they will have the advantage of retiring with their assets protected. The advantage here is by defining the correct course and speed, the client who is nearing retirement will not have his assets destroyed by a market correction or some other unforeseen event.

The person who is retiring or retired can reposition assets to more completely ensure those assets will support them in normal times as well as crisis. The mere fact these assets are protected is the focus of the peace of mind we seek, retired, or not.

What are some of the reasons why people do not choose to preserve their Assets?

This is a good question. The answer is this: watch one hour of TV, or listen to one hour of radio. We are told to buy everything from new cars to home gyms to stocks and gold. There are even commercials telling us NOT to preserve our assets, but trust everything to the stock market. The mindset is this: the party never ends, there is always something for free or some new trinket to make our lives perfect. Taking a hard look at where we are in life, and making adult choices is not promoted in the popular DNA of our times.

You can add to that cognitive dissonance of thought the influence of the Donut Shop Geniuses, the rich uncle, and the TV Financial preachers. Taking the steps to preserve assets is work, and it requires the right kind of coaching and leadership.

The choice to embark on this is not easy. It flies in the face of all of these pressures. The common reticence to make changes follows in the normal momentum of life. Greed and impatience play a role, too.

How do you help your clients through this?

I help my clients by analyzing where they are and getting them to tell me where they want to go. Sometimes this is, for the client very challenging. All too often they have different expectations, plans, and divergent anxieties.

If this is the case, my job is to get them to focus on what they can agree on for now. If this is not the case, my job is to help them see this future more clearly, and then plug in the financial, and legal tools to get them on the right track.

In many cases, their own preconceptions and other financial training will hinder them. Fear of the unknown is a very powerful trap. My job is to tell them not to fear this, but to see it as a challenge, in a happy time where we get to make choices that are all ours, and not governed by a boss, job, or even the requirements of raising children. It's YOUR time let's have some fun with it!

Are there issues other than financial that has to do with preserving assets?

Mental and Emotional Health are irreplaceable assets. One of the biggest issues overlooked by people who are in retirement and nearing retirement are the emotional and mental stressors. This is intimately tied to anxiety about not just money, but the life changes retirement brings.

It is my job to make sure that by preserving financial assets that this anxiety is removed from the mix of other changes. Many advisors focused on remaining 'accumulators' do not take into consideration the underlying anxieties about money and continued lifestyle.

Part of my job is to recognize that protecting mental acuity, emotional health, and relief of anxiety is part of 'protecting' my client. Emotional wellbeing is an asset we need to protect.

Failure to reposition assets to protect them and provide the guaranteed income clients need is an often overlooked facet of maintaining the integrity of the entire 'asset', known as the client, the spouse and the beneficiaries of the estate.

What do you feel are the biggest myths out there when it comes to preserving assets?

How many stars are in the sky? The biggest myth is that you cannot prudently preserve your assets and grow assets at the same time. This is just a sales approach used by stockbrokers and many financial planners to get retirees and soon to be retirees to leave most of their money in stocks bonds and mutual funds. All too often 'bonds' and variable annuities' are promoted as safe havens.

The myth is easily debunked. The question is not being asked correctly. The preservation of assets is like having a national park or nature preserve. By 'preserving the asset' the plan is not to make the asset dormant. It is to stake off part of a bigger set of the financial portfolio from devaluation. By making this 'National Park' or "Nature Preserve' of our indigent funds, we are grooming them for future use, and keeping them prospering no matter what goes on outside of the borders of our 'Preserve'.

When we discuss the use of certain types of financial products to do this the stockbrokers and many financial advisors mock: 'you can't make money in those things'. By contrast, I demythologize this by reminding the potential client 'You might not make 30-40% like you can in the stock market, but you can only lose ZERO. Can the stockbroker guarantee you will never lose ZERO?'

Another misconception is that 'preserving assets' is about financial assets only. While there are many myths about who needs legal work done (wills, powers of attorney, trusts), the fact is, most of us need something done. That is an issue I tackle head-on. Not having powers of attorney and the right legal documents is sometimes more of a threat than having your portfolio not properly protected.

What are some common misconceptions around the retirement planning industry?

The most common misconception, in my opinion, is that our employer plans, 401ks, 403bs, etc. are true planning tools designed by the Plans to guide us and protect us. The opposite is true, they ratify the mantra that we have to risk our money in the Wall Street Casino to have a good retirement. The financial planning industry is only too happy to promote this idea. Look at it this way. The stock market and its derivatives are a labyrinth of arcane rules, and unpredictable tides of supply, demand and emerging technology. In most cases, people in the workforce are tied to this model by their 401ks, 403bs, etc. Very little real planning goes on, it's just check the box and cross your fingers.

It is my job to get prospective clients to:

a. Earlier in their career to diversify away from the stock market only model, and to use good non - market-related accumulation tools to bolster the base of their financial plan.

b. Protect their plans and long-term goals with appropriate types and amounts of life insurance.

The often promoted idea that we should only buy term insurance from our employer is a HUGE common misperception.

What are some of the most common fears about achieving guaranteed income for life?

1. The plan won't grow fast enough to give me the income I need.

2. This is too good to be true, what if the company goes out of business?

3. The company keeps my money if I die and there is money left?

4. I read something on the internet.

5. I saw a TV commercial.

6. My brother said his broker makes him 20-40% even when the market crashes.

7. My banker said indexed annuities are not good.

How can people who are nearing retirement or in retirement get past these fears?

The first thing they can do is meet with me, and bring their goals and anxieties with them to the discussion.

They need help, and they have come to the right place. The first item of business is to ask questions that test the knowledge and trust level.

After inventorying all of their concerns, misconceptions, and fears, I address them, one at a time. If they are visual learners, I use my whiteboard to map out their fears, and address each one head-on, with facts. If they are numbers people, I get their specific questions, write them down, schedule another meeting and then distill the fears in terms of numbers, history, facts, and actual results. If they are more emotional than either of the two types of learning above, I use metaphors and concepts to calm fears; drawing them out as to what causes they far, and how what I am discussing can alleviate those fears.

Once that is done, I know there is some kind of track to run on.

I will tell all prospective clients that it is their money and their decisions.

I let them know there are no dumb questions nor concepts. The main thing is to deal with these fears one at a time.

Most commonly what bothers one spouse will not be a concern of the other.

What other perceived obstacles do you see that might be preventing people who are nearing retirement or in retirement from seeking the help of a Financial Advisor?

In my experience, the first concern is CAN I TRUST THIS PERSON?

Everything else flushes out from that perception.

The client who is concerned about cost often has been burned by being overcharged and underserved. I address this by telling them my business has no fees, that I am paid by the companies with whom I am contracted, and that at no time will I charge them a fee. I also tell them that I only am compensated when a person moves forward to being a client.

Some people are concerned about the length of meetings. I always tell people at my workshop that it is their time. The meeting will last as short or as long as they want it to. This is true whether it's the first meeting or the 25th meeting.

I think many people are afraid that when they walk in they will be hit with a battery of questions and asked to fill out a questionnaire that is 10 pages long and be asked for referrals. I do not operate this way. I ask simple questions, things they will know the answer to. It is very low key and conversational.

Cost and time and trust are all tied together. My job is to let them know neither is a concern. Whether they become a client or not I am trustworthy, and will not waste their time or money.

What pitfalls or common mistakes do you see your clients making on the road to achieving peace of mind in retirement?

From my perspective

1. Not saving enough. Too many people I have seen have not saved enough. Absent a 401k plan, too many entrepreneurs have not opened a Roth IRA, SEP or even bought permanent life insurance with an accumulation feature.

2. Staying too long in the market. Too often near-retirees or retirees are seeking that 'last big push' from the market before they cash out and place money in safety. Sometimes they are rewarded. Too often, seeking that last 10-20% they fail (witness 2001-2002, 2007-2009) and forfeit safety and a 4-5% return for a 30-40% loss.

3. Using retirement funds as a piggy bank. Taking loans and surrenders to buy a car, go on a vacation or even put in a home improvement is a sure fire way to deplete a retirement account, pay unnecessary taxes, and prolong having to work.

How can these pitfalls and or mistakes be avoided?

1. Place funds where they avoid unnecessary taxation and fees. Fees can be portfolio killers and do not minimize risk.

2. Save systematically. Even if you have a 401k, open a Roth IRA or IRA and fund them at a rate you can sustain. This builds redundancy and diversification. One often ignored aspect of retirement is the impact of taxes, and the cost of healthcare. Building a tax advantaged income stream becomes more apparent as one forecasts these intractable costs. Using life insurance, an indexed annuity or something NOT a stock-bond or mutual fund builds an extra layer of emergency funds, safety, and liquidity.

3. Say "NO" to kids. Do not deplete your retirement funds to pay for kids bad decisions.

4. Given today's' low-interest rates, if you need a new car or new roof or home improvement, finance it. Do not use retirement funds for temporary needs.

Share an example of how you have helped a client overcome these obstacles and succeed in achieving peace of mind in retirement.

Back before the financial collapse of 2008, I was working with a client who had about 3 years to go before retirement. He and his wife had amassed quite a bit of money in their

401ks, and IRAs. They had some life insurance through work, and had done no estate planning.

When I met with them they had been told by their financial planner that everything was on track. When they asked him about some of the trouble they were reading about from overseas problems as well as some issues with the collapse of a local bank, the financial planner told them that 'all economic outlooks are good, and with this year being an election year, well the stock market is always up in an election year".

They had attended one of my workshops where I educated the attendees on the need to 'take some money' off the table' regardless of market performance. Since my advice was contrary to what they were told by the 401k advisors at work, and their current financial planner, they were curious to hear what I had to say.

During the course of our conversation, I discovered they had an 'in-service' distribution available to them through their 401k programs. I asked if their advisor knew about this. They said he had never asked. I asked about life insurance. He had never mentioned that. I asked about their wills and powers of attorney. He had never mentioned that. "What," I asked them did he mention?

"Putting money into a variable annuity." They said.

I told them to come back next week and I'd have a proposal for them.

Setting aside the argument of their advisor as a 'bad' idea, I decided to provide these prospective clients with a plan to, first of all, protect their retirement assets.

When we met the following week, I recommended they take the maximum amounts of In-Service Distributions their 401ks. After analyzing their need for 'income replacement' should one of the pass away unexpectedly I recommended a permanent life insurance policy on both of them. Lastly, I recommended they get their wills, and powers of attorney done through the program of LegalShield, which my office carries.

The first thing we did was get the 401k funds moved to fixed indexed annuities. This plan provided a premium bonus, and did two things for them: (1) protected their funds from market loss, and (2) provided a 7% compounding guaranteed growth income purposes. At this point, I had protected 60% of their income from market loss. The rest of the 401k funds had to remain in the employers' accounts.

A byproduct of moving these funds to this indexed annuity was to provide what can be called a 'Multigenerational IRA' option for them. By doing this, we ensured that if both of them passed away their children could 'inherit' these funds without immediate taxable events. Their current 401K did not allow that option.

Later that year, when the market crashed, the funds in the 401K, and the Roth IRA through their advisor lost over 40%.

However, the bulk of their retirement funds DID NOT LOSE A DIME, and the income account still went UP by 7%! Throughout the remainder of the crash, which ended at a low ebb in March of 2009, they NEVER LOST a DIME! By the end of 2010, their income accounts had GROWN by 14%, and their investment had begun to add to the amount protected, plus their bonus.

In the ensuing years, they have had to use their Powers of Attorney for incidents both routine and crisis. When the wife had a bad auto accident, and it didn't look like she would make it, the life insurance in force removed THAT anxiety, and they could focus on her recovery.

They are both now retired. They used every tool I put in their toolbox. Thankfully we never had to do a death claim, but if we had to, the lifestyle they had and the retirement they planned and the funding of their children's' education would have continued.

I am proud of this case; the plan this couple placed into action saved them financially, emotionally, and provided long-term peace of mind not just to them but to the entire family.

What inspired you to become a Financial Advisor?

People often ask me, "how did you get into the financial planning business?"

I did not know it at the time, but it started on Sunday morning at about 2 a.m. At the time I was an executive officer in an artillery battery. My commander was on the phone.

"Lt Scheiber," he began. There was an awful silence. "Get into your class "A"s and meet me at the Orderly Room." Before I could ask why, he hung up. I got dressed and made the drive over to the barracks. All of the lights were on in our Battery area. The rest of the battalion was dark. Upon entering the orderly room, I found the First Sergeant, the Chaplain, and my Battery Commander all in their Class "A" (dress uniforms).

"Sergeant Langdon died tonight." The commander began. "He drowned in Lower Douglas Lake. We are going over to inform his wife. Saddle up." We drove over to their quarters. His wife and three children were in bed. The air was oppressive, the rain had ended but the humidity and fog hung in the air.

We rang the doorbell several times. Finally, a disheveled young woman answered the door, shaking off sleep and not a little bit of worry. As soon as she opened the door, and saw three officers, one of them a chaplain, she backed away from the door, speechless, murmuring 'no. no. no. we were going to retire!'

In the hot, smelting dawn. the awful meeting concluded. My commander, drawn and grim, turned to me. "You are now responsible for her and the three children. I've decided to make you her Survival Assistance Officer."

I was stunned. I knew nothing about 'Survival Assistance'. I was about to learn. What I learned sticks with me to this day.

It was my responsibility to transfer this young family to 'civilian life'. That meant getting all of her Army benefits, survivor benefits, social security benefits paid to her. In addition that meant settling all civil issues; filing the will, getting life insurance (both Army and private insurance) paid out, as well as getting them moved to their home of record. This experience taught me the difference between a family that planned and a family that has done nothing.

Years later, when I was getting out of the Army, my father remembered my experience. He had a friend who was the regional general agent for the Knights of Columbus. I drove from Huntington to South Bend to see him, and before I knew it, I was working as a Fraternal Field Agent for the Knights of Columbus!

The untimely death of sergeant Langdon had a lasting effect on me. Even though I was still just starting out, my commitment to life insurance and making sure people had powers of attorney and wills done were the keys to my passion for the business.

What drives me is the knowledge that most of the people I meet have not prepared for retirement. They do not have their key funds set aside and protected, they do not have their wills and powers of attorney completed, and most of them have no life insurance. The service I provide addresses these issues.

Because I have personally seen the consequences of bad planning, or no planning, these experiences fuel my passion to match clients up with the plan that will result in the most joy and peace in their retirement years.

The best way to contact me is through my website at www.srins.com. There you will see years of newsletters and blog posts, as well as the dates, times, and locations of my seminars.

My retirement workshop. titled 'Rethinking Retirement' is a 70-minute presentation that covers Taxation of retirement benefits, minimizing taxes on IRAs and other deferred retirement accounts and ways of covering Long-Term Care without buying LTC Insurance.

Please share a lesson you learned early on, that still impacts how you do business today.

When I went to work for the Knights of Columbus, my first General Agent, John Stackowicz, taught me that my job was to make sure that if a family member or a member of the Knights of Columbus died, that we, as Fraternalists would be there with a check for that family, helping them.

He said 'there will be a lot of people with their hands out. You will be the only one there handing out money, providing peace of mind."

I see my job now in the same fashion. I can tell you that when my clients retire, I am the person there with a guaranteed check for the rest of their lives. I have never forgotten the financial peace of mind my mother had when my Dad passed. He had set everything up so that she would never have to worry about running out of money.

I see these lessons as unrepeatable rules of life.

If someone wants to know more about preserving their assets, so they can they can have guaranteed income for life, how can they contact you?

The best thing a prospective client can do is contact me at (952) 649-0504, or through my website at www.srins.com. They can also personally email me at pscheiber@srins.com. There they can see the schedule for all of my workshops, and obtain the information necessary to register for a workshop, read dozens of articles I have published, as well as see informational videos and educational pieces.

As this book goes to press, there will be several opportunities to meet with me and obtain a free signed copy of the book. Interested people can attend a workshop, or meet me at my book release party. Details on that will be posted to my website at www.srins.com.

For information on a free consultation, please contact me by phone, email or through my website. To sign up for my monthly newsletter the "St. Anselm Report" please call, email or visit my website and request to be sent the print or e-version of the "St. Anselm Report."

The best way to contact me is through my website at www.srins.com. There you will see years of newsletters and blog posts, as well as the dates, times, and locations of my seminars.

My retirement workshop. titled 'Rethinking Retirement' is a 70-minute presentation that covers Taxation of retirement benefits, minimizing taxes on IRAs and other deferred retirement accounts and ways of covering Long-Term Care without buying LTC Insurance.

JAY BROWN

Investment Advisor
Strategic Financial

Email: jbrown@stratfinan.com
Website: http://www.stratfinan.com
LinkedIn: www.linkedin.com/in/jay-brown-sf
Call: (415) 789-3700

Jay Brown is a financial advisor who specializes in working with people retired or nearing retirement. Jay has been providing investment advice and serving Bay Area residents for over 35 years. His planning process starts with an in-depth analysis of a client's goals and objectives. After an evaluation, Jay makes recommendations and works with his clients to implement a financial plan. The end result is to assure the client's financial plan meets his or her goals. Mr. Brown works mostly on a referral basis, with satisfied clients recommending his services to others.

Jay has an extensive network of experts on his team to assist his clients to navigate through the complexities of their financial and estate planning needs. Jay's passion in his work is evident; to help solve the many financial and emotional issues that pre-retirees and retirees encounter. Some of the professional services and planning strategies covered are asset protection, capital preservation, income distribution, required minimum distributions and estate planning.

Jay is an Investment Advisor Representative and holds the Series 6 Securities License, the California Life and Health License, as well as the Series 65 Investment Advisors License. His practice has thrived, and Jay is fortunate to help an ever-increasing number of people every year.

Mr. Brown is involved in a number of community events. He is a member of the Local Chamber of Commerce and has been the president and long-term member of two different Toastmasters organizations in the area.

SIMPLE STRATEGIES FOR A SAFE AND SECURE RETIREMENT
By Jay Brown

Tell us about Strategic Financial, the people you work with and the types of situations they find themselves in when they come to you for your help?

I help people who are nearing retirement, or who are already in retirement, to lower their investment risks, so they can have more freedom and peace of mind in knowing that they will never outlast their money, no matter how long they live.

People come to me, usually from my comprehensive, popular Retirement Planning Workshops throughout the San Francisco Bay Area, or by referrals. Most people mention to me that they do not really understand many of the basic concepts before they attend my Workshops; they confide in me that they are "novices" or "beginners".

It is gratifying to me to know that after they listen to the 5 or 6 key financial strategies that I cover in my Workshops, they understand much better what they have to do in order to have a safe & secure retirement. I almost always can help with the 2 big problems that people face entering retirement; the risk of outliving their money, and the consequences of not being able to take care of themselves (i.e., needing long-term care) and the huge costs that could occur from that.

When someone has benefited from a planning session with me, a "cloud" seems to have been lifted from over their head. People can go about their daily lives with more "peace of mind" and confidence. The transformation for one of my clients, who has become a good friend, was simply amazing. It seemed that he was a new person, with a completely different outlook on life.

What are the advantages of lowering investment risks for people nearing or in retirement?

As people age, they should take less investment risk. I regularly mention that it takes more in gains to compensate for prior stock market losses. For instance, if an investor loses 30% in their portfolios (which is less than what happened in 2008-2009), then they would NEED to get a return of 43% over a period in time just to break even (it does not matter what arbitrary numbers are used in this example).

Many clients that I meet for the first time usually have no idea how much risk they are taking with their investments. Sometimes people initially come into my office for the first time, they are in their eighties, and they have over 90% or more in small-cap stocks. No wonder they have sleeping problems at night (I would too if I were in their situation!)

Like anything in life, sometimes one cannot put a price tag on "peace of mind" as it relates to one's quality of life. Lowering a client's investment risk may not adversely affect the long-term rate of return on someone's investments. Instead, it can help to avoid the many negative experiences that people feel that have to live through.

By lowering taxes and different risks, pre-retirees can increase the value of their portfolios and help ensure a larger nest egg in retirement, as well as leaving a larger estate to their loved ones.

When it comes to lowering investment risks, what are some of the biggest myths out there?

There seem to be many myths in the financial world (and for many things in life, for that matter). One is that an investor must accept a lower rate of return in order to get more safety. This is not always the case. In my Workshops, I discuss a number of financial products that provide attractive returns with an emphasis on safety.

I have heard Financial Advisors and Stockbrokers say to people in their eighties that "they are in it for the long haul". All kidding aside, as people progress into their retirement years, the investment strategy should be one of "capital preservation" versus "capital accumulation" (that was probably prevalent in their younger years).

This is not to say that retirees should not be concerned with the growth of their investments. It is still important to sustain a minimum growth rate (such as keeping up with the rate of inflation, plus maybe another 2-3%), and to have some of their portfolios in stable (preferred) stocks.

Some people feel that they want some "excitement" from their investments, whether it be in the stock market, real estate, or some other investment. Wealth building can be methodical and takes patience. If this process is not very "exciting", then someone should take that up in their personal lifestyle.

What are some common misconceptions around the Finance industry?

One popular misconception is that people typically view Financial Advisors/Planners as fairly much the same, and think that they can take their financial concerns or problems to any Advisor and expect solutions. I provide financial solutions as it relates to someone approaching retirement or already in retirement. Some planners may only be able or may only be educated to work with millennials, for instance. So, consumers may need to seek out the area of expertise and the specialty of the Financial Advisors, especially as it relates to certain age demographics.

Another common misconception that I see is that most consumers may not be aware of the many regulatory and compliance procedures that are currently in place in order to protect them when working with a planner and investing. It seems that with the passage of times, these procedures get even stronger, which is important for the integrity of the financial services industry. For example, the much anticipated Department of Labor's Fiduciary Rule went into effect last year.

What do people nearing or in retirement fear about even attempting to lower their investment risks?

There is a general tendency for people to continue on with their "game plan" throughout their life, thinking they do not need to change anything as the decades pass.

So, many take the same investment risk well into their retirement years as they did when they were working. Plus, many of their friends also reinforce this idea of staying with the status quo, of not changing. So, I usually go through a discussion about "Capital Accumulation" versus "Capital Preservation".

Also, many people that I initially work with have fears that they may not be able to sustain their lifestyle well into retirement. Once we talk about and bring out into the open the various risks, including investment risks, that person begins to see that they should start the process in order to have a comprehensive, strategic plan in place.

The number one reason that people do not take action (whether it is to come to our initial meeting for the first meeting, or to fund an appropriate investment), is procrastination. This can be a debilitating mindset to have, as people can sometimes feel overwhelmed with what they know that should do. Change sometimes is not easy to do and can be met with resistance.

It is in the small, simple, and incremental steps that, over a period of time, can result in significant progress and tangible results. The planning process can take many months, or even years, depending on the client and the size of the estate.

How can people nearing or in retirement get past those fears?

I know that the best way for someone to get past those fears is to make the process as enjoyable as possible. If someone has an invitation to my Retirement Planning Workshops, why not go and be educated in a lively Workshop that covers the half-dozen key principles, make some new friends, and get a nice dinner.

There are some great books on these subjects (I also give out a suggested reading list at my Workshops), as well as informative & special public television shows.

The important thing is to be empowered to take that first step. The steps can be incrementally small, though I like to make steady progress in helping a client to reach their goals.

What other perceived obstacles do you see that might be preventing people from seeking the help of an Investment Advisor?

It is not unusual for me to sense that the person that I encounter for the first time may be a little "embarrassed" by how little they know about finances. Sometimes, people feel self-conscious about this, even though they really should not.

I majored in "Finance" when I was in college/university, and I have been in the Financial Services industry since 1981, so I have a lot of experience, knowledge, and competence to provide financial guidance.

So, here is the analogy. If my automobile broke down, I would be virtually helpless (this is almost embarrassing for me to admit, but it is true). So, I depend on someone who has a specialty in that (i.e., a good mechanic, in this situation).

It is the same with a good Financial Advisor/Planner; let someone help you who has the training and experience to reach your financial objectives.

The average person trying to do this himself or herself just does not have the training and experience, and it is not fair to compare this person to a professional Financial Advisor.

Still, other people are unclear as to the compensation to the Advisor.

For me, it is always about doing what is in the best interests of my client (i.e., the Fiduciary Rule). So, I look at whatever the compensation is, it will be a mere fraction of the value I provide for my client.

In general, compensation does NOT come out of the client's account on insurance plans (and is instead paid directly from the insurer) and DOES come out of the client's account (i.e., "off the top") for assets under management. Lastly, there may be fees for comprehensive financial or estate planning, though I do not do much of this in my day-to-day practice.

What are some of the common mistakes you see people nearing or in retirement make?

One common mistake that I see as people start to prepare for retirement, is not "seeing" the potential issues that could prevent someone from having a safe and secure retirement.

One is not having enough monthly income, on a guaranteed basis, coming in every month, for the rest of someone's life.

Another would be the inability to handle (emotionally, and more importantly, financially) the consequences of declining health and long-term care issues.

Another common mistake is not knowing the basic planning process, nor an understanding of the cost (I addressed the cost model in the previous section). Full transparency should be the rule at every encounter, and the customer needs to do some reading of any material that is provided.

How can these pitfalls and or mistakes be avoided?

As alluded to, consumers need to know their options, an understanding of reasonable expectations, and the costs involved. Fortunately, many safeguards are in place in the financial services industry. Like almost any other profession, it can be just the "few bad apples" that gets the attention in the news.

So for the consumer, to be educated with some of the basics, so that there is a knowledge baseline, would be helpful.

Share an example of how you have helped people nearing or in retirement to overcome these obstacles and succeed in lowering their investment risks?

A few years ago, I was referred into a family living in San Francisco. After a considerable amount of time and long meetings in the Discovery Phase, we outlined a financial game plan that emphasized preservation of capital. They have friends who experienced recent stock market volatility, as well as uncertainty about other aspects of their future.

Now, this family has more confidence and certainty about their future. This not only affects these individuals but also their friends and the people they come in contact with.

What inspired you to become an Investment Advisor, what's your backstory?

I started in the financial services industry with a major Life Insurance Company in April of 1981.

I was only a couple of years out of college/university when I entered this business. My last year at the University I was introduced to the lessons learned of Dale Carnegie, Napoleon Hill, Earl Nightingale, among other greats, and I was immersed into the power of positive thinking.

This was then carried over to when I started in the business and found my passion as I enjoyed helping people, and liked the process of matching the best product (and/or strategy) to meet my clients' needs. Early in my career, I was pleasantly surprised that so many people needed and benefited from our products.

What are your final thoughts for anyone who is considering lowering their investment risks?

It could be the difference between retiring with peace of mind and retiring and needing to watch one's budget every month, because there may not be enough money.

I find that many times there is no need to have the level of risk that people in retirement have.

The idea is to avoid the "big mistakes", that includes the possibility of losing 30%, or more, of one's portfolio. A good financial professional can assist in finding the appropriate risk level for an individual's assets.

What's the most important thing people nearing or in retirement should consider when evaluating an Investment Advisor?

I would say the Investment Advisor's professional education, experience, and whether they specialize in certain areas of expertise. It takes several years to really understand the business and to select a specialty.

There is mandatory continuing education as well. Someone who has been in the business for decades has both the experience of how to assist people with their objectives and also the formal education (in order to maintain their different licensees).

If someone wants to lower their investment risks, feel confident and have peace of mind that they'll never run out of money during their retirement, how can they connect with you?

I have a free report about how to get started that you can download by going to my website www.stratfinan.com.

Or, you can simply call (415) 789-3700 ext. 101 and either request this free report, request a complimentary consultation session, and/or to get on my invitational list for my Retirement Planning Workshops.

Whatever way someone decides to contact us, they will know what to expect every step along the way in this straightforward process.

I hope to have an opportunity to serve you!

DANIEL FISHER, RFC

Registered Financial Consultant
Sole Owner, Fisher Financial Group, LLC

Email: dan@fisherfinancialgroupllc.com
Website: www.fisherfinancialgroupllc.com
LinkedIn: www.linkedin.com/in/danielfisher328
Facebook: FisherFinancialGroupLLC
Twitter: financialpro123
Call: (847) 205-9300

Daniel Fisher has been assisting individuals and their families who are retired or nearing retirement for the last 35 years. Mr. Fisher started his career as an accountant and transitioned into advising individuals on growing and preserving their assets conservatively while paying the least amount in income taxes.

Dan now specializes and focuses in working with federal employees across all agencies of the federal government and is passionate about helping them navigate their somewhat complex benefits.

Dan's expertise is in high demand, and he hosts CSRS and FERS pre-retirement classes locally in the Chicago area. More importantly, as a financial planner for federal employees, he has helped hundreds of individual federal employees through the entire retirement process.

Dan has been a featured guest speaker on ABC's Windy City Live TV and Fox32Chicago TV as "Dan the Money Man" and also on America's Wealth Management Show on WIND 560 AM radio.

Dan is a Registered Financial Consultant (RFC) and an Investment Advisor Representative with Fisher Financial Group, LLC, a Registered Investment Advisor firm and works as a fiduciary in the best interest of his clients. He holds a Bachelor of Science in Business Administration degree from Roosevelt University and majored in Accounting and Taxes.

ATTENTION FEDERAL EMPLOYEES!
By Daniel Fisher

Tell us about Fisher Financial Group, LLC and the federal employees approaching or contemplating retirement you work with.

At Fisher Financial Group, LLC Dan Fisher specializes in the retirement needs of federal employees and their families. Dan's ideal client is a federal employee approaching or contemplating retirement, who seeks his assistance and expertise, will implement the strategies he recommends and one who will ultimately develop into a long-term, mutually beneficial relationship.

The biggest problem I solve for my client is putting together all the pieces of the retirement puzzle so that my client has a clearer picture of what's involved and how to proceed towards a successful retirement. Simply put, federal employees have a terrific benefit system. I break down their benefits and explain all the ins and outs of what they're entitled to such as their FERS and CSRS pensions, their Thrift Savings Plan options and Federal Employee Group Life Insurance.

Federal employees are allowed to carry certain benefits into retirement besides their pensions such as health insurance, life insurance, long-term care insurance and dental and vision. To avoid confusion and figure out the benefits a federal employee is entitled to in retirement we start with the basics of what they should keep or not keep or make adjustments based on their needs.

By going through this planning process my clients grasp a better understanding of what they should do upon submitting their retirement paperwork. Their financial future then is more predictable, and they gain confidence and peace of mind going into retirement.

What are the advantages of creating a financial plan for federal employees approaching or contemplating retirement?

The major advantage of creating a financial plan is that it helps people, especially federal employees, see the big picture and set long and short-term life goals, a crucial step in mapping out their financial futures. When they have a financial plan, it's easier to make financial decisions and stay on track to meet their goals.

Another advantage is that it can build confidence for many by knowing that they have taken that extra step in formulating a plan that can have a huge effect on the rest of their lives.

Finally, creating a financial plan gives people peace of mind that they can live a comfortable retirement and, if not, what they have to do to change things so that they can.

What do you feel are the biggest myths out there when it comes to creating a financial plan?

The biggest myth when it comes to creating a financial plan is the perceived notion that it's only for wealthy people who have a lot of money and that it's too expensive. Part of this misconception may be rooted in the fact that people often lump financial advisers into the same category as other professionals, such as attorneys, who often charge expensive retainers. Thus, many people have the mindset that "I can't afford a financial advisor" or "My situation is too small" for a financial advisor to even consider working with me. Nonsense! I take an interest in helping everyone I work with whether they work in the boiler room of an office building or the operating room of a VA facility.

Price is seldom an issue for me because people generally see the value of what I bring to the table and know they can rely on me for unbiased, objective advice. The fact is that financial planning is beneficial for everyone because it helps you balance living for today while preparing for the future.

Another myth is that many people feel they have plenty of time to plan for retirement. It's really never too early to start planning. In fact, the longer you wait, the harder you'll have to work and the more you'll have to save for retirement.

Having a plan gives you direction and shows you your options. Without a plan, how can you even be sure when you can retire? Do you know what you'll need to cover your most basic expenses and where those funds are coming from? Do you know if you can afford to take up a new hobby, travel more, or pay off your mortgage? Do you know when would be the best time to start drawing Social Security? If you plan to work part-time after retirement, do you know what the earnings limits are if you take Social Security before your full retirement age? Do you know how your income taxes will be impacted by withdrawals from your retirement accounts as opposed to your taxable investments? And how do you know that you won't outlive your money? A financial planner can help you with all of this and much more.

What are some common misconceptions around the Finance industry?

There are several misconceptions I come across when counseling federal employees. One major misconception is that many federal employees assume that all financial advisors in my industry are the same and are knowledgeable about the federal benefits system. This is simply not the case! In my estimation there are less than 5% of advisors nationwide, myself included, that actually have the training and deep understanding of the federal system. Because of this how can a federal employee depend on any advisor he's been working with in the past to chart a retirement course that excludes knowing about the FERS or CSRS pension benefit that the employee is entitled to?

Another misconception is the mindset of many who say "I don't need a financial advisor." Let's get real. Of course you do! When you have a tax problem you call a CPA to resolve it. When you buy a house or have a legal issue you hire an attorney. And when you prepare for retirement you call a federally trained financial advisor. Why? Because you're making some very important decisions that will impact you for the rest of your life! Also, you're developing a relationship with a trained advisor who will guide you as your retirement picture unfolds and as your situation changes.

What are some of the most common fears about creating a financial plan?

A common fear about creating a financial plan for most people is the anticipation of not having enough money to retire or that they will outlive their money. They believe they can't afford to lose any money, and their fear of making a poor decision prevents them from making any decision at all.

Another fear is that data shows that many investors have not yet recovered from the emotional toll that the financial crisis of 2008 created. But this fear is leading to more and more people being unprepared for the reality of retirement, and this results in creating a financial plan in the first place.

It's obvious that most of us lead busy lives, and it does take a commitment in time to create a financial plan so this could be yet another fear many federal employees face.

How can federal employees approaching or contemplating retirement get past those fears?

Fear is usually a response to uncertainty and the potential for financial pain, so when you have more certainty and knowledge about your finances, fear is less of a factor in your life.

By taking the time to discuss your fears and concerns with a financial advisor, you can help overcome those obstacles by creating roadmaps that will guide you to a financially secure retirement and placing potential strategies in proper context.

For example, I usually perform a risk assessment to help guide my clients in making smart investment decisions through diversification. By not "putting all their eggs in one basket" my clients feel relieved that they don't have to pay as much attention to the direction of the market or the news of the day. They can then focus more on living their retirement years with a lot less stress knowing that someone is looking out for their best interests.

Regarding time commitment, I take a step by step approach in working with my clients. I will meet with them as many times as needed until the objective is achieved by creating and implementing their financial plans. I realize that a lot of my new clients have never met with a financial advisor in their lives so baby steps are taken to make sure we're working as a team for their common goal of financial independence.

What other perceived obstacles do you see that might be preventing federal employees from seeking the help of a Registered Financial Consultant?

The most common obstacle I see that might prevent federal employees from seeking my help is trust. Trust means everything in any type of relationship, whether we're focusing on romance, family or finances. People have to trust me before they're willing to implement any recommendations I make. This actually is quite normal in our society today. After all, there are many shady advisors out there that give my profession a bad name. Trust is thus earned after people work with me over a period of time and they then gladly refer me to their coworkers, friends and neighbors.

Another perceived obstacle is cost. I constantly get asked the question: "What's it going to cost me?" or "What's in it for you?" Frankly, it's going to cost them nothing to meet and get a plan established. I truly do get the satisfaction of knowing I've helped, and perhaps changed, a person's life for the better.

What are some of the common pitfalls and mistakes you see federal employees approaching or contemplating retirement make?

There are numerous pitfalls I see, but the most common one is that federal employees are not getting well informed about important decisions that will affect them for the rest of their lives. Information may come from fellow coworkers who wrongly advise them about what they did for themselves. Obviously, this is not objective advice when taking into consideration all the intricacies of the federal employee's benefits.

Another common pitfall is many federal employees don't believe they can retire comfortably or simply can't do it at all. They may be resigned to thinking they'll have to work for the rest of their lives or have very few years in retirement.

Yet another mistake I see with federal employees approaching retirement is, in my opinion, that they invest too aggressively in their Thrift Savings Plan and personal investments. I'm shocked to find out that they never changed their investment allocations since they were hired! They have to realize that they don't have as much time to make up losses in the event of a market downturn as when they were in the early stages of their careers.

How can these pitfalls or mistakes be avoided?

By getting educated! All federal employees should learn the rules of the federal retirement game so they know how to play. This can be accomplished through the many classroom educational workshops that I've hosted over the years or simply just reading up on the subject. There are numerous great books, articles and videos on the subject from seasoned professionals. Also, a financial advisor can be a tremendous resource to them to help answer any questions they have and explain strategies or financial concepts they want to know more about, within the context of their own financial circumstances.

Crafting a retirement plan will give a clearer picture as to the federal employee's time frame for retirement. I almost always run several "what if" scenarios to alleviate the fear of not being able to retire by offering options given the federal employee's circumstances. Also, a risk assessment will reveal how much volatility they're willing to endure in retirement with their Thrift Savings Plans and other personal investments.

Share an example of how you have helped federal employees approaching or contemplating retirement to overcome these obstacles and succeed in creating a financial plan.

As I mentioned before I've assisted hundreds of federal employees plan for their retirement. This would not have been possible if they hadn't attended the classroom training workshops I have hosted. I truly feel that a classroom education venue helps many people overcome these obstacles by setting up the groundwork for creating a financial plan afterward. I bring in the best of the best speakers, many of whom have worked for the federal government or have served in the military and are intimately familiar with the federal benefits program. The speakers are engaging and bring forth material that is easily understood and comprehended without being too technical and boring. By attending these workshops attendees can see firsthand the professional caliber of the presenters and the information put forth and, therefore, are eager to meet with me to help them explore and better understand their benefits.

I have a different approach to planning than most financial advisors. While many financial professionals talk about financial planning they're often only really focused on your investments. I'm different because I look at the entire financial picture, and not just one piece of the pie. I ask many questions and probe into a person's background including their health and family history.

Why do I do this? Because having a conversation about this reveals when and how they should start their pension benefits and what survivor option they should consider. Also, that information equips me on how to advise the federal employee as to when and how they should turn on their Social Security benefits. After all, if a person does not have longevity in their family perhaps they should start their benefits sooner rather than later. In general, I advise people that the number one thing they should do before retiring is to get a complete physical. This may sound simplistic but this way they'll have a clearer understanding of their overall health and be better prepared for making the right financial decisions that will affect them for the rest of their lives.

To summarize, I look at all the pieces of my clients' financial puzzle and help put them together in a way that achieves their goals. By using this approach I develop long-term relationships with my clients who usually hire me several years before retirement, and we work together through their retirement years and beyond. I can't form that type of relationship with my clients unless they like me, trust my judgment and appreciate my interest in them.

What led you to become a Registered Financial Consultant and Sole Owner, what's your backstory?

As an accountant for several years after graduating from college, I always liked working with numbers. Believe it or not, I actually enjoyed putting financial statements together and preparing tax returns. But besides all this, I felt that it came up short. Why? Because I was dealing with history rather than looking ahead and planning for my clients. I was inspired by many of the financial world gurus, such as Warren Buffett and Jack Bogle, and became more interested in financial and investment planning for my clientele. I started preparing plans and realized how many of my clients were ill-prepared for their retirement and offered them suggestions for getting them on the right track.

The road that led me to specialize in working with federal employees was not an easy one, but it turned out to be a great learning experience. Several years ago I met a federal employee who I tried to help but couldn't because of my lack of knowledge in the federal benefit system. That person wound up going elsewhere to another advisor. I then realized that I simply had to get training to better equip myself in situations such as this. Over time I studied up on the federal benefit system and started hosting complimentary educational federal employee workshops locally.

One particular workshop was onsite at a Veterans Administration location in their auditorium. I was surprised that over a hundred people came to hear the presentation! I then realized that there was a huge demand for quality information and people were eager to learn more about their federal benefits system. More importantly, they were anxious for my help to figure out how these benefits applied to their particular situation. Being an analytic person with an accounting background I began the process of taking their information and preparing financial plans focusing on their needs. I continue to do so today with all federal employees regardless of their position, wage grade or GS level- everyone is treated equally.

What's most important for federal employees to keep in mind when evaluating a Financial Consultant?

The most important thing is that they should do their homework on any advisor they intend on hiring. To start off, they should ask if the advisor is a fiduciary and one who will look out for their best interest. In today's world, this is a requirement, yet many advisors do not follow this doctrine. They should also inquire about how the advisor is compensated and how often he will meet with them to review their financial situation. Ideally, work with a fee-based advisor if possible to avoid conflicts of interest. The initial meeting would be a good time to get these questions answered and resolved so that there are no surprises later on.

Typical signs to watch out for when shopping for an advisor include looking into the background and education of the advisor. Has the advisor been in business for a long time? Does the advisor have a financial background or was he a used car salesman just last month? Being competent and educated on federal benefits is, after all, not something that can be learned overnight. It can actually take years to be proficient in having a deep understanding of this complex system.

Last but not least, the federal employee should ask the advisor if he/she is knowledgeable in the federal benefits system. By knowing the federal system the advisor can create a much more comprehensive plan that integrates personal assets with the federal benefits the employee is entitled to.

What are your final thoughts for federal employees approaching or contemplating retirement when considering creating a financial plan?

I would tell federal employees not to go it alone or think that they can do it all themselves when considering creating a financial plan. I love the human resources people in the federal government system, but they are not there to give you objective advice or tell you what to do in planning your financial future. Take the time to learn about your benefits so you can maximize them to the fullest potential. Attend an educational federal retirement workshop. Seek the advice of a seasoned professional who is knowledgeable in the federal benefits system and who can crunch the numbers for you. Last, but not least, envision what your retirement years will look like. Do you want to travel, spend time with your family, golf or volunteer? Only by planning will your dreams be achieved. Dream big!

If someone wants to create a financial plan, achieve peace of mind and proceed toward a successful retirement, how can they connect with you?

I offer free periodic federal employee educational workshops in the Chicago area throughout the year for anyone interested. A complimentary 1-hour consultation at a later time at my office is offered at the end of the workshop for anyone interested in taking the first step towards gaining a better understanding of their benefits and build upon what they have learned at the workshop.

When we meet, and after your federal retirement options are reviewed, you will receive a personalized report offering a comprehensive approach to your retirement plan. At that time I will offer some suggestions, ideas or recommendations on how to enhance your financial outlook. Whether you implement my recommendations or not we always part as friends. I've found that this approach works best and is a no lose proposition for anyone interested in working with me.

There is no one-size-fits-all solution when it comes to your retirement planning. I take your unique situation into account and build a plan centered around your needs. After all, retirement is a challenge for everyone, but only a crisis for some. What will yours be? I encourage you to get your federal benefit analysis report and see where you stand. There is a well known saying in my industry: "People don't plan to fail-they fail to plan." Since failure is not an option for most let me show you how to plan for your success.

You can call my office at (847) 205-9300 or email me at dan@fisherfinancialgroupllc.com to find out when our next workshop will be held or if you would like to set up that initial one on one complimentary, no obligation one-hour consultation at my office.

TIMOTHY A. KLEIN

Retirement Income Planner
Bay Harbor Financial Group, LLC

Email: avonleyklein@yahoo.com
Website: www.bayharborfinancialgroup.com
Call: (616) 293-6315

Timothy Klein was born in Sparta, MI and grew up on an apple farm where his favorite activity was driving the family tractor. He attended Sparta High where he was all-conference in football, broke three records in the hurdles and placed in the state hurdles final his senior year. After graduating high school he attended Michigan State University where he attained a business degree.

After college, he chose to help his dad run the family farm during which time he helped engineer and patent a fruit vending machine. Even though most of the business was wholesale Tim found himself enjoying the interactions with customers on the retail side. He didn't know it at the time, but he would soon pursue a position that involved working with the public on a daily basis.

Planning for retirement was always important to Tim and he began searching for the perfect solution for his family. He was surprised by the amount of misinformation and empty promises in most of the retirement vehicles, however, he did find some answers to what he was looking for. When Tim discovered these principles about 7 years ago he decided that he must inform others of this and immediately chose a career in retirement income planning.

MASTER YOUR RETIREMENT
By Timothy A. Klein

Tell us about Bay Harbor Financial Group, LLC, the clients you work with and the types of situations they find themselves in when they come to you for your help?

AARP did a survey and the #1 retirement concern was "outliving their savings."

Most of the folks we meet with aren't sure how much retirement income they will need or whether they are on track to meet those needs.

Bay Harbor Financial Group was formed to help folks navigate their retirement years by providing safe retirement vehicles that preserve principal while maximizing income.

What does a safe retirement look like?

Peace of mind through principle protection is key. Warren Buffett was asked for advice on investing and he gave 2 principles that all investors should adhere to:

Rule #1 - Never lose money.

Rule #2 - See #1.

If you lose 20% in a given year you must make a 25% return the next just to break even. Most of the folks I talk to want a reasonable rate of return with the least amount of risk possible.

What do you feel is the biggest myth out there when it comes to having a safe retirement?

Safety = Low Returns. Many people believe they must take risks to achieve growth. This simply is not true. Some of the wealthiest investors in the world choose strategies that offer great upside potential but eliminate most of the downside risk. Tony Robbins lays out a number of these options in his latest book; "Money, Master the Game." We also share his enthusiasm in the pursuit of maximizing returns while simultaneously protecting principal and annual gains.

What are some common misconceptions around the Finance industry?

There are more actively managed mutual funds than stocks; in fact, there are over 13 trillion dollars invested in mutual funds. The sad reality is that 96% of mutual funds fail to beat the S & P 500 over a 20 year period giving investors average returns of 2.54% between 1993-2013 compared to 9.28% with the S & P 500. That's an 80% difference. The reality is that Wall Street makes money off of actively managed mutual funds but the public rarely sees any benefit in this activity.

What are some of your client's most common fears about safe retirement?

Outliving their money is the #1 fear but nobody enjoys losing money anytime especially since they worked so hard to accumulate it. This is why there are trillions of dollars deposited into bank CD's; people don't want to take a chance of losing their principle. Long-term care is another major concern that can devastate retirement savings at over $91,000/ year. The odds of needing long-term care for a couple is 91% according to USA TODAY and it should be addressed in every retirement plan.

How can folks get past these fears?

Education is key; understanding the difference between risk vehicles and safe vehicles is key. Also, a clear understanding of what you are trying to accomplish is necessary for fine-tuning your retirement strategy. Some people just focus on returns rather than focusing on future income structure, principal protection, and long-term care risks. Returns are important and the necessary fuel for most retirement plans but they are just one element of a balanced approach to proper planning.

What other perceived obstacles do you see that might be preventing people from seeking help from folks like yourself?

Trust; most folks are not sure who to trust. Banks, their broker, an insurance agent, a friend or family member. The second obstacle is what strategy; CD's, annuities, mutual funds, bonds, stocks, gold, silver, or commodities. There is an overwhelming amount of information in both of these areas; enough so that some people just give up and do it themselves or stick with the 1st strategy they began with.

What are some of the little-known pitfalls or common mistakes you see people make on the road to preserving their nest egg, without ever having to run out of money?

Income planning is the most important element in most retirement plans yet most folks I sit down with do not have a plan for income. Most folks I sit down with want to retire and maintain their lifestyle yet their current plan lacks a solid structure that guarantees a certain amount of income at a specific age.

How can these pitfalls or mistakes be avoided?

Hope for the best but plan for the worst is my motto. The closer you are to retirement the less of a loss you can absorb so principle protection is a major priority. Income riders are available on some investment vehicles at a 7% guaranteed annual increase and can provide peace of mind by avoiding income fluctuations. Some income riders even double the income for long-term care expenses helping reduce exposure in that area.

Share an example of how you have helped someone to overcome these obstacles and succeed in preserving their nest egg.

I have a client that had seven accounts with four different companies for a total of $612,000 of value in mixed mutual funds, life insurance and annuities prior to meeting with me. Her goal was to simplify or consolidate her money, have the safety of principal and income. I consolidated the previous funds into one company with two products into a fixed indexed annuity with an immediate bonus of $61,200 for a total account value of $673,200 (tax deferred) and lifetime income guaranteed. My client was happy to consolidate and therefore make her retirement simpler with tax-deferred growth and 100% secure against market loss.

What inspired you to become a retirement income planner?

For many years I have been inspired by Tony Robbins author, entrepreneur, and philanthropist. He is one of the nation's #1 life, business and personal development strategist. He's been called upon to consult and coach with some of the world's finest athletes, entertainers, Fortune 500 CEOs and even presidents of nations. Ultimately, his book Money Master The Game gave me the passion to do what I do.

Tony interviewed and did research with 50 of the world's most brilliant financial minds who gave him their opinion on how to achieve financial freedom for the common person in America. There is at least one chapter in the book about indexed annuities and how they guarantee income and safety, all derived from some of the world's best financial minds. Wow, that astounds me! With this being said, I was truly inspired because of Tony's book and it gave me the perfect solution to solving peoples financial worries.

One of the common mistakes that I see folks make is taking on too much risk in their retirement years. I always demonstrate what's called "The Rule Of 100" to my potential clients. To demonstrate that rule, you take your age and subtract it from 100 and the number that remains means that you should not have any more than that percentage in a risk type of investment. For example: 100 - 70 (age) = 30 or 30% (maximum at risk).

Even Warren Buffett, known for his incredibly unique ability to find undervalued stocks, says that the average investor should never attempt to pick stocks or time the market. In his famous 2014 letter to his shareholders, he explained that when he passes away, the money in a trust for his wife should be invested only in indexes so that she minimizes her cost and maximizes her upside.

I now have the statistics and proof to show how to plan and redistribute their retirement without having the misconceptions and empty promises that so many folks have from their current or previous financial planner.

What's the most important thing folks should consider when evaluating a Retirement Income Planner?

Does he or she understand what I'm trying to accomplish and are they familiar with the tools necessary to get the job done? Most planners focus on returns only and don't spend hours talking about what problems can arise and how to avoid them. Experience is a must have in these critical areas because one mistake can be extremely costly at or near retirement distribution age.

What are your final thoughts for folks who are considering preserving their nest egg without ever having to run out of money?

Is there a floor underneath your money right now; in other words; are you protected from the ups and downs of the stock market? If the answer is no you owe it to yourself to at least take a look at the options which can give you this floor of protection.

If someone feels they want to have safe retirement, so they can preserve their nest egg without ever having to run out of money, how can they connect with you and what will happen when they do?

What we do is find out what your main objectives are, address them carefully, and provide the safest solutions to them in a "no cost, no obligation" plan.

VIVIAN TOOMAIRE, RFC

President
VNMutual Solutions, Inc.

Email: info@vnmutualsolutions.com
Website: https://vnmutualsolutions.com
LinkedIn: https://linkedin.com/company/vnmutual
Scheduling: https://vnmutualsolutions.com/contact-us
Facebook: https://www.facebook.com/VNMutual
Twitter: http://www.twitter.com/vnmutual
Call: (847) 794-8897

Vivian is a well-respected wealth expert throughout the Chicagoland and surrounding areas. Her presidency at VNMutual Solutions Inc. began in 2013; where her dedication to the success of others has come to light.

VNMutual was founded with the intent to provide strategic financial guidance aimed at helping clients reach, and even surpass their financial potential; in the most efficient way possible. Vivian not only understands the difference, yet also understands the importance of conducting business to the fiduciary standard; thus recommending to her clients only what is in their utmost of interest.

Additionally, she is a member of the Society for Financial Awareness; a national non-profit organization whose goal is to eliminate financial illiteracy in our communities through proper financial education. Vivian values giving back, therefore; philanthropy in various aspects is a meaningful part of her life.

As a licensed financial professional, she not only takes the time to thoroughly educate her clients on an ongoing basis; yet she also provides financial education to employers, their employees, members of our community, and beyond. She works closely with her accomplished and dedicated team of licensed professionals, combining her knowledge, experience, and aptitude for research; to tailor personalized advice that allows each client an optimum opportunity at potentially reaching their loftiest financial goals – both personally and in business.

The quality of advice she provides to every client is consistent with how she advises her own family and closest friends. Her clients' success truly is her success.

THE EFFECT OF
FINANCIAL EFFICIENCY
By Vivian Toomaire

Tell us about VNMutual Solutions, Inc., the individuals and business owners you work with and the types of situations they find themselves in when they come to you for your help?

At VNMutual, we provide extensive solutions for both the personal side of your finances as well as the business side. Our goal is to help you maximize your financial efficiency; allowing you the optimal opportunity to attain, if not exceed your financial goals. "Efficiency is doing better what is already being done". – Peter Drucker.

On the personal side, we have several clients whose initial concerns relate to losing a large portion of their retirement savings due to market fluctuations and often times are also concerned about potential tax implications if they were to move their money to less risky alternatives. The majority of these clients simply want to ensure that they have a comfortable retirement without having to worry about losing money or not having enough to last. Often times, they also want to have everything structured so they are able to leave money for future generations as well.

On the business side, aside from each company having their own unique set of circumstances and goals; many of our clients - be it small or large: share a common goal of maximizing the efficiency of their company. This not only applies to the day to day business activities, but especially to the financial aspect of business. Interestingly enough, many small businesses do not offer employee benefits to their employees. This is often because of the perceived expense involved. On a larger scale, large companies are often paying much higher fees than necessary, have increased complexity while maintaining benefits administered, and may even have low enrollment rate in certain benefits – all of which negatively impacts financial efficiency.

Our independent contractor and other self-employed clients, just like any of our other clients; have concerns of their own - and beyond the basics, often aren't sure where to start. Regardless to the industry – be it transportation, childcare, real estate, entertainment, construction, or other industry; the countless retirement account types, insurance choices, and other benefit options available; make selecting which ones are best for you a cumbersome task.

Without naming anyone; think of the countless celebrities, lottery winners, executives, and other professionals that went from an abundance of financial wealth, to living paycheck to paycheck – or even worse, bankruptcy. Do you think that's the end goal these people had in mind? Always remember; it's not about how much money you make or have, it's about how well you manage it. With that said, clients of ours in this category often seek ongoing, continuous advice with reference to how much money to set aside for taxes, government fees, spending, the out of pocket expenses for benefits, ensuring a proper amount is contributed towards retirement, and much more. It is not uncommon for us to work side by side with clients' talent managers and agents.

And last but certainly not least, several of our clients from a combination of the categories mentioned (above); desire to create a legacy that will never be forgotten. Of course people of all asset and income levels can leave a meaningful legacy of their own; however a majority of our clients who share such aspirations, typically have a higher net worth and often aim to either allocate a significant portion of their estate to charitable organizations or already have their own foundation. The fact that there are additional complexities and concerns involved goes unsaid when aiming to give back and make a momentous impact in our world.

Our team of licensed professionals works closely together with you to implement the most ideal plan to allow you an optimal opportunity at attaining your loftiest goals – whether it may involve you, your family, your business, philanthropy, or a combination thereof.

What are the advantages of increasing financial efficiency personally and in business?

The advantages of increasing your financial efficiency, in all aspects are vast.

Implementing the right strategy can result in growth, principal protection, income, providing for future generations or even for a cause that is near and dear to your heart – the list goes on. You work hard for your money; make your money work hard for you. And the sooner you start, the more impactful the future outcome will be. Be it earned or inherited, do you really want to let money you could have; slip away instead? Absolutely not.

Additionally to the above, there are additional advantages for business clients. For example, offering an excellent employee benefits package to your employees and doing so as efficiently as possible; not only helps you retain your most talented employees but it allows you to do so at a minimal cost – regardless to what percentage you're contributing.

So, on the business side; whether we're helping you implement a new employee benefits package tailored to your specific needs, increasing the efficiency of existing employee benefits, expanding the benefits offered, or educating you and your employees about benefits available and how to enroll; the end result can lower overall costs, decrease employee turnover rates, increase retained income, increase productivity, increase employee benefit enrollment rate, simplify maintenance, and much more. It's a mutual win for your company and for your employees; which is ultimately the best scenario.

What do you feel are the biggest myths out there when it comes to increasing the efficiency of finances?

Providing employee benefits are expensive and unnecessary. This seems to be a common myth and it's understandable that employers, especially small businesses perceive benefits as being too expensive to offer. Interestingly enough however, most business owners do not realize even a smaller benefits package is ultimately better than none at all – and can be more affordable than you may think. Additionally, studies show a strong correlation between offering employee benefits and finding and retaining good employees – not to mention productivity. Benefits and other perks make people feel appreciated, valued, helps increase their feeling of self-worth, and can even incentivize them to perform better. Insight to consider: *"Clients do not come first. Employees come first. If you take care of your employees, they will take care of your clients". – Richard Branson.* It's no surprise that so many people are opting for slightly lower pay in exchange for an excellent benefits package.

Once you hire a financial professional, you never need to change anything again. This is another surprisingly common myth. I can't tell you how many people I've met that have insurance policies that no longer fit their needs, investment portfolios that need to be reallocated, beneficiaries that need to be updated and so on.

The most important takeaway is that as the years go by, life happens. Marriage, children, college, large purchases, retirement, unexpected expenses - are all just a few of many. Things evolve and so do our needs. What once may have been fine may no longer be ideal. There are many aspects people don't even think about, so it's important to have a financial professional who understands these areas and puts forth the effort to keep things up to date with you, on a regular basis. And that's a key element of our firm; since we view our client relationships as lifelong ones, we take the time to review our clients' accounts face to face so we stay on the same page, for years to come. If you have an advisor, when is the last time you heard from him or her? If you're in the majority, the answer is; too long!

What are some common misconceptions around the Finance and Insurance industry?

Some people think vaguely listing some of their accounts over the phone, without providing financial documents for review, is sufficient for them to get an actionable recommendation at that very moment. I'm sorry to say but it doesn't work that way. Understand that it is our responsibility to do our due diligence and understand your financial circumstances to the extent that will allow us to make accurate recommendations. This includes analyzing your statements and an investment of time on your part to openly discuss essential details. Without having necessary elements in place, how can you possibly expect to get advice that's in your best interest? It's simple, you can't.

Another misconception is a *"finances are simple, I can do it alone"* mentality. While in some cases, this may be true; a second opinion never hurts. It's common for people to realize that saving towards retirement is important, for parents with children to realize that they should have life insurance, along with other financial basics. However, what people do not always realize, is that their finances can be more complex than it seems.

Think about it for a moment. With just the two examples I mentioned, the options are almost endless. With a countless choices to select from in your retirement account and around a dozen different types of life insurance policies to select from – not to mention the various ways to structure them and the different benefit choices that come with each, that all vary from company to company; the potential combinations of choices can be exhausting. How will you know if you are truly selecting the best choices for you? The fact is; without proper advice, you don't.

When it comes to increasing the efficiency of personal and business finances, what are some of your client's most common fears?

Ending up with less money than you started off with is a fear for many. It's natural to have doubts, questions, and concerns when making major decisions in life. This goes for anyone, whether you're in business or not – you want to know that whatever decisions you're making, are the right ones.

Another fear, especially in business is related to *new technology*. Small business or large company; when you're accustomed to doing things a certain way, the idea of change can be intimidating - even if there is a reason necessitating change. Just think about how much technology evolved over the past few decades alone. A lot, right?

What should people do to get past those fears?

This is a good question. When you're exploring major options, such as those related to your finances, make sure you understand the differences between how things currently work versus what will change after implementing new solutions. Never feel afraid to ask questions, clarify answers, and simply make sure you understand details of what to expect once you move your money.

When you're making the decision to utilize new technology, it's important you'll be up to par with the ever-changing regulations, compliance, privacy demands, and any other areas pertaining to your industry. Additionally, it's important to consider simplicity and ease of use when it comes to maintaining and accessing benefits administered – for both employers and employees.

Having a single platform, for example, is a great way to save time by allowing everyone to have their own single login username and password, without having to create separate logins for each benefit. You and your employees have better things to do with your time - Focus on your business and let your employees focus on their jobs, instead. *"Time is money"* *– Benjamin Franklin.*

What other perceived obstacles do you see that might be preventing individuals and business owners from seeking the help of a Financial Professional?

Lack of time is huge. Let's face it, we're all busy people. How many times have you put certain things on your to-do list, only to postpone it yet again? Countless times, right?

Perhaps you're putting off getting financial advice, purchasing an insurance policy, exploring your long-term care options while you're healthy, making updates to or reviewing your investment portfolio, trust, estate plan, insurance policy, and other financially related documents. The list is endless.

We've all been there, but realize that for various reasons, it's important to make it a priority and set aside time to meet with your financial professional and get everything in order – before it's too late. *"Time waits for no one" – Yasutake Tsutsui*

When it comes to increasing the efficiency of personal and business finances, what are some of the common pitfalls and mistakes you see individuals and business owners make?

When moving your money from account to account or from place to place, it is absolutely imperative that you do so correctly. Especially with the various options you have on how to move your money, I cannot stress how easy it is to make a small error that can cost you big time. Literally, a significant chunk of your money goes down the drain just that fast. It can be in the way of taxes, penalties, perhaps a recent change in regulation you did not realize, or in some other form. Don't fall into this trap – seek advice and do it right.

Not being open about your financial circumstances with your financial professional is another potentially costly mistake. You may think it's only necessary that your financial professional disclose information thoroughly, yet it's important for you to disclose your financial circumstances in detail too.

Consider this; how can you expect a financial professional to provide accurate advice to you if you have not fully disclosed your financial situation? During our analyzation process, there are specific factors we take into consideration that go beyond the numbers. With this said, details of your full financial picture allow us to provide proper and accurate financial advice that is truly in your best interest.

How can these pitfalls or mistakes be avoided?

I sort of touched on this a moment ago, but my first piece of advice to you is to get an adviser and follow the advice. Work with a financial professional you feel good about, one you trust. And don't hold back when it comes to sharing your current financial circumstances, your goals, your needs – because this is the person who is going to be by your side for years to come, guiding you to realizing your financial aspirations.

Share an example of how you have helped individuals or business owners to overcome obstacles and succeed in increasing the efficiency of their finances.

I'll share an example of a small business client of ours. A husband and wife both in their 50's who also happen to own a service related business together; have 2 children, 4 grandchildren, and a total of 7 employees - including themselves and their 2 married adult children. Aside from mandatory benefits such as workman's compensation; there were no additional employee benefits in place. Everyone purchased and paid for individual medical insurance and premiums out of pocket – which happens to be the most expensive option, especially if you do not qualify for plans through the marketplace.

When it came to retirement, the way everyone did things varied significantly. Some employees didn't save at all, one had a retirement account open and contributed regularly, others had only a savings account, both adult children put money towards their retirement accounts only occasionally, and the husband and wife contributed fairly consistently into their existing individual accounts for retirement. Being referred by another one of our existing clients, this couple contacted us to find out about potential options available to them. We set up our initial consultation on-site and together went over various details of both their company and personal circumstances for the owners and other employees as well. We also took into consideration certain lifestyle expenses.

In the end, we helped cut costs of medical insurance premiums, implement the standard dental and vision coverage, automate retirement contributions, create additional peace of mind through disability insurance, life insurance, various other wellness and lifestyle benefits, and more. Not only were we able to provide quality benefits while keeping company expenses at a minimum; we were also able to offer other optional benefits which reduced both occasional and recurring personal costs that various employees would normally pay for anyway or in some cases were unable to afford otherwise. Additionally, employees are also positioned to better attain their personal financial goals and meet their estate planning needs. For example, the owners had additional concerns we also resolved; regarding the seamless and efficient transfer of wealth to future generations, not just personally yet with regard to their business as well.

They've since grown their company, hired 3 additional employees, and during our recent review meeting said they couldn't be happier they made the decision to meet with us. It is a rewarding feeling for me, knowing our clients are truly satisfied.

What led or inspired you to become a Financial Professional, what's your backstory?

Since I was a little girl, I've always loved helping people. Growing up, I was always a saver and eventually amassed thousands of dollars by the time I was a teenager - which I eventually ended up investing. I always knew I would either end up in the health field helping patients to feel better or as the founder of a financial firm helping people maximize their finances. I believe that every human being deserves the opportunity to reach their optimum, in each aspect of life. Finances are no exception. So, here I am, fulfilling my passion for helping others.

What are the most important things people should consider when evaluating a Financial Professional?

Working with a financial professional who is acting as your fiduciary is necessary. This means that your financial professional is acting in your best interest. It is tremendously important because if hypothetically there are two different potential solutions, both of which are suitable for you; yet one is better for you and the other will pay the financial professional more – which one do you want your financial professional to recommend to you? The one that's best for you, right? Absolutely! And that should always be the *only* option. *Realize: "The financial industry is a service industry. It should serve others before it serves itself". – Christine Lagarde.*

The numerous advantages of selecting an independent financial professional from an independent financial firm should also be taken into consideration. To name a few - unlike captive financial professionals, independent financial professionals do not have quotas to meet, have greater fee transparency, and are not bound to any particular family of funds or just one company's insurance or financial offerings. At our firm, we feel these are important factors because having vast access to a limitless range of potential solutions to select from, enables us to formulate the ideal blend of solutions that are best for you and your unique needs.

What are your final thoughts for those who are considering increasing the efficiency of their finances, personally and/or in business?

Seeking and implementing proper financial advice is a very precise, detail-oriented and personalized process. And during this process, it's important that you feel comfortable – rather than pressured. Know that you are worth having your financial professional make an effort to really get to know you, what you aim to accomplish, and more. Furthermore, you deserve to have him or her take the time to not only make recommendations to you, but also to ensure you have an understanding of how the solutions work, what you can expect, and other essential facts that educate you and ultimately make you a well-informed client.

Always clarify your understanding and keep an open channel of communication between you and your financial professional. And with endless changes, developments, and advancements, in the financial industry and beyond; don't be afraid to explore potential options and opportunities that may be available to you. You never know what new things you'll learn and how you may improve your financial efficiency and beyond. What's really nice is, to get started, all you have to do is ask. *"You get in life what you have the courage to ask for".* – *Oprah Winfrey*

If someone feels they want to increase the efficiency of their finances and maximize their fullest financial potential, both personally and in business, how can they connect with you?

The first step will be to schedule a consultation with us, so we can learn more about your needs and goals. The easiest way for you to do this is to visit us on the web at www.vnmutualsolutions.com and click the **"Get Started Now" Button on our homepage**. From there, simply select Initial Discovery Consultation, a date and time on our calendar, and schedule yourself in. It should take a few minutes or less. It's that easy.

Once you're scheduled in, you can expect to receive an email confirmation with the details of your meeting, where you'll also have the ability to upload financial statements and relevant documents using a link to our secure portal. You'll also receive a text reminder, so while scheduling, you'll want to make sure you put your cell phone number as opposed to your landline.

During your initial consultation, if you haven't already uploaded your financially related documents, we'll gather a copy of these along with other critical information necessary for us to make accurate recommendations. This meeting typically takes about half an hour but can be more or less depending on your needs. You can expect to schedule your next meeting during this time.

After your Initial Discovery Consultation with us, we'll analyze the information we've gathered along with the financial statements and other relevant documents you've provided. During this time, we'll strategically tailor your solutions. This process typically takes about a week, at which time you'll have your second meeting with us to go over details of your recommendations.

From here, depending on the types of recommendations we will be implementing, the process can take anywhere from a few days up to about a few weeks to complete.

Once you become a client, you can expect to hear from us on a regular basis. Routinely reviewing your finances and your evolving circumstances is just one of many ways we ensure we keep you on the most efficient path to attaining your very own financial goals – whatever they may be!

ABOUT THE AUTHOR

Mark Imperial is a Best Selling Author, Syndicated Business Columnist, Syndicated Radio Host, and internationally recognized Stage, Screen, and Radio Host of numerous business shows spotlighting leading experts, entrepreneurs, and business celebrities.

His passion is discovering noteworthy business owners, professionals, experts, and leaders who do great work, and sharing their stories and secrets to their success with the world on his syndicated radio program titled "Remarkable Radio".

Mark is also the media marketing strategist and voice for some of the world's most famous brands. You can hear his voice over the airwaves weekly on Chicago radio and worldwide on iHeart Radio.

Mark is a Karate black belt, teaches kickboxing, loves Thai food, House Music, and his favorite TV show is infomercials.

Learn more:

www.MarkImperial.com
www.ImperialAction.com
www.RemarkableRadioShow.com